God Wants a House

God Wants A House

Lance Lambert

LANCE LAMBERT MINISTRIES

Richmond, Virginia, USA

ISBN: 978-1-68389-015-7

www.lancelambert.org

Preface

Through the two books of Chronicles Lance Lambert reveals God's purpose for the creation of man from before the foundation of the world. God wants a dwelling place, a home for Himself which means that it is not just a matter of being saved or filled with the Spirit. It is that believers are to be living stones built together for a habitation of God in the Spirit. It is the place where God is at home, the place where He reveals Himself, the place from which God rules and reigns, and the place where all the beauty of the character of God is to be forever expressed.

This is something tremendous when you consider what He has to work with—worthless, insignificant, sinful creatures. How amazing is the grace of God that He has not only forgiven us, declared us to be righteous, but it is to bring us into this relationship with Himself for all eternity.

This purpose of God for man is not only costly, there is great conflict over it. Satan has through the ages tried to destroy it, but Jesus said: "I will build My church and the gates of hell will not prevail against it."

May the Holy Spirit give revelation to all who read this book, that there will be a desire and hunger within each one to be a part of this glorious house.

These messages were given in 1974 in Richmond, VA.

Contents

Preface _____ 7

God Wants A House _____ 11

The House is Costly _____ 37

Now is the Building of the House _____ 71

Materials for the House _____ 97

1.
God Wants a House

1 Chronicles 22: 2–19

And David commanded to gather together the sojourners that were in the land of Israel; and he set masons to hew wrought stones to build the house of God. And David prepared iron in abundance for the nails for the doors of the gates, and for the couplings; and brass in abundance without weight; and cedar-trees without number: for the Sidonians and they of Tyre brought cedar-trees in abundance to David. And David said, Solomon my son is young and tender, and the house that is to be builded for the Lord must be exceeding magnificent, of fame and of glory throughout all countries: I will therefore make preparation for it. So David prepared abundantly before his death.

Then he called for Solomon his son, and charged him to build a house for the Lord, the God of Israel. And David said to Solomon his son, As for me, it was in my heart to build a house unto the name of the Lord my God. But the word of the

Lord came to me, saying, Thou hast shed blood abundantly, and hast made great wars: thou shalt not build a house unto my name, because thou hast shed much blood upon the earth in my sight. Behold, a son shall be born to thee, who shall be a man of rest; and I will give him rest from all his enemies round about; for his name shall be Solomon, and I will give peace and quietness unto Israel in his days. He shall build a house for my name; and he shall be my son, and I will be his father; and I will establish the throne of his kingdom over Israel forever. Now, my son, The Lord be with thee; and prosper thou, and build the house of the Lord thy God, as he hath spoken concerning thee. Only the Lord give thee discretion and understanding, and give thee charge concerning Israel; that so thou mayest keep the law of the Lord thy God. Then shalt thou prosper, if thou observe to do the statutes and the ordinances which the Lord charged Moses with concerning Israel: be strong, and of good courage; fear not, neither be dismayed. Now, behold, in my affliction I have prepared for the house of the Lord a hundred thousand talents of gold, and a thousand thousand talents of silver, and of brass and iron without weight; for it is in abundance: timber also and stone have I prepared; and thou mayest add thereto. Moreover there are workmen with thee in abundance, hewers and workers of stone and timber, and all men that are skillful in every manner of work: of the gold, the silver, and the brass, and the iron, there is no number. Arise and be doing, and the Lord be with thee.

David also commanded all the princes of Israel to help

Solomon his son, saying, Is not the Lord your God with you? and hath he not given you rest on every side? for he hath delivered the inhabitants of the land into my hand; and the land is subdued before the Lord, and before his people. Now set your heart and your soul to seek after the Lord your God; arise therefore, and build ye the sanctuary of the Lord God, to bring the ark of the covenant of the Lord, and the holy vessels of God, into the house that is to be built to the name of the Lord.

I want to share with you on the two books of Chronicles. I know that some people find the books of Chronicles chronic. They start in I Chronicles with all those long pedigrees and genealogies, and by the time they have waded through ten chapters of it they are just about finished. Then again there are people who feel they cannot quite understand why we have I and II Chronicles anyway because after all nearly the whole of it is found in I and II Samuel and I and II Kings. So why have Chronicles redoing the whole thing? Why not just have I and II Samuel and I and II Kings? But when God repeats anything, it is vitally important. God never wastes words or time. God is always looking for something with a very real objective, and Chronicles is one of the most vitally important books in the Bible.

There are certain books which are the interpretation of other books and these books are therefore in a special position. For instance, there are two books that come immediately to my mind. One of them is Deuteronomy, which is the second giving of the law or the fifth book of the Bible, and is in fact a going over of everything we find in Exodus, Leviticus and Numbers. But it is absolutely vital because the book of Deuteronomy goes to the heart of all that God has been doing in Genesis, Exodus, Leviticus, and Numbers. A new element is added, which is there all the time, but perhaps we had not noticed. And the finger of God is put upon it and it is defined, and attention is focused upon it. God has done all this because He loves His people and wants them to be a vessel for Himself.

Another book that goes over the same ground as Matthew, Mark and Luke, which are historical records, is the Gospel according to John. Of course, John's Gospel is also historical, but it is written as an interpretation of the preceding three books. Therefore you get the whole Gospel built upon eight claims of I AM and eight great signs.

Chronicles is just like these books. It goes over the ground all over again and this time it focuses our attention upon the heart of the matter. It is as if God is saying, "Now then you have gone through all this before, but we are going to go right back again to the beginning and recap, and then I am going to point out to you what lies behind everything."

Chronicles covers all the ground that is found in the two books of Samuel and the two books of Kings. The theme of Samuel and Kings is the king and the kingdom, and the whole of that history is all about the way God brings in His king and His kingdom.

Chronicles Reveals the Purpose of God

Chronicles goes over all that ground once more and says there is something even more vital than even the kingdom. God brings in

His kingdom in order that His house may be built. So the theme of the two books of Chronicles, Ezra and Nehemiah, which are in the Jewish reckoning, are considered to be one book. Behind the coming of the king, the kingdom, and the throne of God is this purpose of God's heart to have a home for Himself, to obtain an elect people, to produce living stones and then build them together upon the right foundation into a holy temple in the Lord. In other words, the theme of I and II Chronicles is the eternal purpose of God. It goes right back to Adam, through all those genealogies, goes on beyond Solomon to the return under Zerubbabel from Babylon, and it is as if God says, "Now the whole of this history is explained in this home." Here is the eternal purpose of God. Behind all these things, behind all these incidents, behind all these reigns, behind all the history of these different saints of God lies the sovereign, eternal purpose of God to obtain a home for Himself or another way—to produce a bride for His Son.

The Possibility of Leaving the Will of God

That is why we have the pedigrees and the genealogies which are very wonderful. But it is not just the question that they are the genealogy of our Lord. It is the fact that God is doing something with people and it is possible to either stay within the center of God's purpose or go out of it. If you go out of the will of God you will not lose your salvation, but you will lose your inheritance. Some people think that Christians cannot go out of the will of God but they can. There are those with the pedigrees, people who started right but went off. And there are others who started wrong and were in an awful mess, but by the grace of God they got right and came into the center of God's purpose—people like Bathsheba, Tamar, Ruth. Other people began very well, had the right parentage, the right pedigree, but went clean out; Esau was one of them. There were others who had the right father and the right mother but they went out of the purpose of God.

Then we have these chapters in Chronicles that have to do with the preparation for the house, the battles that had to be fought, the materials that had to be won, all the laying, as it were, of the ground, the obtaining of things for the Lord in order that the house of God might be built. Then we have the actual record of the building.

After that there are many chapters on the conflict over the house of God. Once the house of God is built then all hell comes out against it to destroy it or compromise it. And we have the record of the way that hell itself comes out to shake it by either a frontal attack which comes at them from without or an internal attack, which is from within in a worldly way or fashion, to undo that work.

In Ezra and Nehemiah, as it was originally, we have not only the conflict and the ruin of the house and the testimony of the Lord but we have finally the recovery in glory.

The theme of Chronicles is the eternal purpose of God. It is as if God says, "Now come with Me. We have recorded all the history of Genesis, Exodus, Leviticus, Numbers, Deuteronomy, Joshua, Judges, Ruth, I and II Samuel, I and II Kings, but now come with Me. This is not really the heart of the matter. You have only seen the outward circumstances, you have only been seeing outwardly, now come with Me. I want to take you right back again to Adam and trace the whole history again. Then I want to tell you the theme that is upon My heart, the theme that has governed a pouring out of grace upon you, the reason there is a way of salvation for you. I want to tell you what it all means. I want you to come with Me to the eternal purpose of God." Of course, when we come to the New Testament we find this again and again.

Genesis and Revelation

I remember years ago when I first discovered this, it was my greatest thrill when to my amazement I found that the first three chapters and the last three chapters of the Bible minutely correspond. All these people who tell us that the Bible is sort of legend and myths, rather wobbly in part, and you cannot trust it completely, I find amazing. The reason it is so amazing is because although everyone has always believed that Genesis should be the first book, there was much discussion about Revelation through the first four centuries of the early church and it did not occupy the last position in the books of the Bible for many years. Sometimes it was put elsewhere but not at the end. Finally, in the fourth century after Christ the book of Revelation was universally recognized as being wholly of God and found its position at the end of the Bible. So it is not as if someone said, "Now then I will sit down and write something which caps the lot." It was the Spirit of God that was doing it.

In the first three chapters of the Bible we find a heaven and an earth (Genesis 2:4). In the last three chapters there is a new heaven and a new earth (Revelation 21:1).

In the first three chapters we will find that time is ushered in (Genesis 1). In the last three chapters there is eternity ushered in (Revelation 21).

In the first three chapters we find Satan entering (Genesis 3:1). In the last three chapters we find Satan being cast out forever (Revelation 20:10).

In the first three chapters we find paradise lost (Genesis 3:24). In the last three chapters paradise is regained (Revelation 21:3).

In the first three chapters earth is cursed (Genesis 3:17). In the last three chapters we have the wonderful words "no more curse" (Revelation 22:3).

In the first three chapters we find only two people, Adam and Eve, man and woman (Genesis 2:23). In the last three chapters those two people have given place to an innumerable company of a redeemed people which no man could number (Revelation 21:3; 22:14).

In the first three chapters there is a garden (Genesis 2:8), and the garden gives way in the last three chapters to a city (Revelation 21:2). Now the city is a garden city but it is still a city.

In the first three chapters we find the tree of life (Genesis 2:9). In the last three chapters we find the tree of life (Revelation 22:2).

In the first three chapters there is the river of life (Genesis 2:10). In the last three chapters the river of life is flowing out to the ends of the earth (Revelation 22:2).

In the first three chapters we find God walking in the midst of the garden once a day. In other words, once a day God visited the garden to fellowship with Adam and Eve and talk with them.

In the last three chapters we find God dwelling in the midst of His own forever. He is not visiting them; He is not just coming in and going out once a day; He is there; it is His home. He has come home. He is there forever. If He goes out, He goes out from among them and comes back to them. This is His home (Revelation 21:3).

In the first three chapters there is an earthly marriage (Genesis 2:21–25). Man and woman, Adam and Eve enter into an earthly marriage till death parted them. In the last three chapters there is the heavenly or eternal marriage. There the Lamb and the wife of the Lamb are in the eternal marriage of which earthly marriage is only a picture, a symbol or an illustration.

In the first three chapters there is pain, sorrow, and death (Genesis 3:16–19). In the last three chapters we find the wonderful words: "No more pain, crying, mourning or death" (Revelation 21:4).

The Three Substances Found in the River of Life

In the first three chapters we find three substances. And in Genesis 2:11–12 there is a tree of life in the midst and a river of life that flows out into four great rivers that waters the whole earth. Then it says, "If you follow the river you will find firstly gold, and the gold of that land is good," which is a very strange thing to say. Then it says, "You will also find onyx stone and a thing called bdellium." So there are three substances—gold, onyx stone, and bdellium. This is quite interesting because first it is near the tree of life, and secondly when we follow the river of life we find these three things.

Gold and Onyx

We have no problem about the gold. But onyx is very interesting because in Exodus 28:9–12 or 28:18–20 the high priest had twelve precious stones on the breast plate and each stone represented one of the twelve tribes of Israel. On each precious stone was engraved the name of the tribe, and he had them on his heart. It was a picture of the high priest bearing the whole people of God on his heart before God. Those twelve names of the twelve tribes were then gathered up onto his shoulders. He had six stones with six of the names engraved on one shoulder and six stones with six names engraved on the other shoulder meaning that the government was upon his shoulders. But the stones on his shoulders did not correspond with the stones on his breastplate which were onyx stone. In other words, the onyx gathered up all the preciousness and qualities of the other stones; it becomes the symbol of them all. So when you follow this river of life you find not only gold but you find precious stones because the onyx stone symbolizes all the precious stones of the Bible.

Bdellium

Now the bdellium is even more interesting. And this word was much discussed by the rabbis in our Lord's day as to what it was. Bdellium is an aromatic plant and when you break it, a white substance comes out. Then it hardens and has an opaque mother of pearl look. In Hebrew it is called the "pearl plant In our Lord's day the rabbis were often describing it as to whether this plant was not actually river pearls. We do not know, but what we have are three substances—gold, precious stones and something which is very much like a pearl. It certainly has the same symbolism of a pearl. You have to break it which means suffering. And out of the broken plant comes its very life blood, and this life blood becomes something like a pearl.

The City in Revelation has Three Substances

Gold

In the last three chapters of the Bible we find a city of incredible beauty, and it is produced out of only three substances—gold, precious stone, and pearl. There is no other substance in the whole of the city, only three (Revelation 21:18–21). The gold is so refined that it is transparent as glass. Not one of you has ever seen gold transparent as glass. What refining! What fire! What affliction that gold has gone through to become transparent as glass so that only the glory of God can go through it. There is nothing to stop the glory of God nor the light of God from shining through it. It is incredibly wrought upon. It is gold of the most precious quality.

Precious Stones

The second thing is precious stones, which are the twelve foundations of the city. And we remember when the God of glory appeared to Abraham, he went out seeking the city which had foundations. And what are these foundations upon which the eternal city rests? They are the twelve precious stones that have come from deep down in the dark places of the earth. How have they been formed? By tremendous heat and pressure in hidden places, treasures of darkness, hidden riches of secret places, says the prophet Isaiah. These have been found by the Spirit of God, brought out and wonderfully wrought upon so that they become a city. Think of that! Gold and precious stones have all been wrought upon in such a way that they become a city compacted together, builded together.

Pearl

And the third thing is the twelve gates which are each of one pearl. The way into the city is everlastingly through a pearl gate, and the way out is everlastingly through a pearl gate. And we know that in Scripture gates speak of government; it is where things were settled in the olden days. The elders would go to the gates and there they sat for judgment and for settling disputes and making things legal and definite so they could not be changed. What a wonderful thing this is!

The Way to Find the Substances

In the first three chapters, these things are not obvious to the naked eye. The only thing that is more obvious is the river; therefore you have to follow the river. If you start with the tree of life and then follow the river of life, you will come to gold. But where is the gold? The gold is all in the silt. It has to be discovered; it has to be mined; it has to be sieved; it has to be fired, but it is all there.

Where do you find the precious stone? Under the very ground you will be walking on. You do not see it with these eyes; it is there but it has to be found, discovered.

Where is the pearl? It is in the water on the river bed. A piece of grit falls into the softest part of the clam and the clam says, "Ouch, I do not like this; I am going to eject this piece of grit.

This does not belong to me. This has nothing to do with my life. This is Satan; this is something that comes from hell. So now I will take all the resources that are within my life and I will put a coat around it and eject it." It puts a coat around it, but the grit stays. Again, another coat goes around it, then another coat, and you can almost hear the clam saying, "Lord, Lord, take this messenger of Satan away from me." It is like the agony of impalement; this is a thorn in the flesh. But the Lord says, "My grace is sufficient for thee." And another coat goes round that little grit. And he seeks the Lord again and says, "Take it away, take it away, Lord." And the Lord says, "No." And another coat goes around it. It is the result of the energy of the life of God in you producing a coat around the grit. The grit is not taken away, but God changes the grit.

The Jade Smiths

Years ago I remember listening to Mildred Cable speaking about the jade smiths of Central Asia and of Peking. She said that she had never forgotten those jade smiths who were known to us, and sometimes for as many as six years they would sit looking and looking at a piece of jade with a flaw in it. And the whole art was how to make the flaw the central part of the piece. Some of you have seen those beautiful pieces of jade in Washington. You will see in one of them that piece of ground in a beautiful piece of jade is a flaw and he has made a bee on the peony. Or he has taken an ugly little piece of flaky grey and made it a frog on the lotus leaf. So the flaw has become the central piece and the source of the reason for the whole. It is the same thing with the pearl.

The city is all there in the beginning of the Bible only you cannot see it with the naked eye. The liberal theologian can scoff at it, but it is all there. And when the Spirit of God opens the eyes of our heart we suddenly find that the beginning of the Bible and the end of the Bible have an extraordinary correspondence and no man did it. The Spirit of God brought these three things together.

I will tell you something even more remarkable. If we take the first two chapters of Genesis and the last two chapters of Revelation we have the beginning and the end of a matter without the fall of man or sin; except perhaps in Revelation 22 where it says, "Nothing filthy or maketh a lie shall enter into the city." Otherwise, we have the beginning and the end of the matter. We have something that God set out to do and the end, there it is completed. Here it is all in a hidden way, and there it is all produced and wrought upon and is something of eternal and incredible beauty.

In chapter 3 of Genesis we have the entry of Satan and the fall of man, sin, the curse, death, and all the rest of it. Then in Revelation 20 we have the end of it. Thank God Satan is thrown into a lake of fire and that is the end of the whole thing.

The Coming of the Messiah

So we have Genesis 1 and 2 and then chapter 3 is the beginning of the parenthesis, a fall into sin—time and the whole tragic story of man and the glory of the story of the coming of the Messiah. There is promise at the very beginning and we follow the story right to the fall of man and the coming of the Messiah. And when Messiah comes, born of a woman, born of David's line, He gives

His life for the salvation of us all. We still have the fall of man, but now we have a redeemed people; but we are still in the parenthesis. But isn't it wonderful when we come to Revelation 20 we are at the end of the parenthesis; finished! The former things have passed away: "Behold I make all things new." Isn't that wonderful!

What Does God Have in Mind for His People

And here is the amazing thing: we do not know what God is really going to do. People say that they find heaven rather boring— just lying around all day doing nothing, sort of an eternal choir. Won't we get rather tired of singing these praises for a thousand years nonstop? Won't we get a little bit weary? There is a misunderstanding of eternity that is a fantasy. Of course, we are going to sing, of course, we are going to praise, but do you think that God, who is the Creator, is going to stop creating? Of course not! This world with all its beauty is a pale reflection of what God originally had in mind for man.

Romans 8 is the whole thing of being subjected to the bondage of corruption. Now we do not know what that means, but it seems somehow or other that these trees and fields, this natural creation was meant for something else originally, but because of the fall of man it lost its object; it lost its purpose; it lost its heart. And the whole thing has been an endless cycle of corruption, vanity, emptiness, and futility, all waiting for the manifestation of the glory of the sons of God. Oh, how wonderful! We do not know what is going to happen. All we know is that the Bible ends with a marriage, and there are only two ways of looking at marriage;

either it is the end or it is the beginning. Some people say, "Oh dear, that is the end." Other people say, "They are beginning life." Marriage is really two things; it is the end of one phase and the beginning of another. Now the Bible ends with a marriage.

You love your Lord, don't you? And the more you discover Him, don't you find it absolutely marvelous? If you get disappointed with believers, you will never get disappointed with the Lord Jesus. There must be something wrong with you if you get disappointed with Him. I have never yet been disappointed with the Lord. I have been disappointed by believers a thousand, thousand times and by myself even more, but with the Lord I have never been disappointed. And there are times when we are in the valley or times when we have mountain top experiences. I remember years ago being given a little book called "The Roof Top Christians." It spoke about the fellow Christians who were greatly inhibited. There were brethren who loved eating. There were drawing room Christians who were the Methodists and loved to be getting on doing things. There were the bedroom Christians where certain folks were fast asleep. Then there were the attic Christians, and there were the roof top Christians who shouted "Hallelujah" all day long because they were filled with joy unspeakable and full of glory.

The point is this, when we begin to see something of the purpose of God it is so wonderful. The Bible ends with a marriage, but God has said: "Now I am not going to tell you what I am going to do in eternity. All I am telling you is that at last you and My Son are together." Even with all these wonderful experiences we have we are only betrothed; we are only engaged. We are not yet married. We are in a state of betrothal; we are actually engaged to our Lord. The marriage supper of the Lamb is still to come. What is it going to be like? We shall be transported out of ourselves. When this marriage is finally consummated, when we really are one spirit, soul and body for all eternity, it is going to be absolutely marvelous. When we look back we will say it was worth it. It was worth every single affliction; it was worth every dark spot; it was worth every single bit of being knocked about by other saints and being built together. It was worth it to put up with so and so and to go through with them. It was absolutely worth it because here we are. We are not just those blessed ones who have been invited to the marriage supper of the Lamb, but we are the ones who are actually the bride herself. Oh, how wonderful!

And we do not know what it will be in the future. We do not know what God is going to do. All I know is that God is the Creator; He does not stop; He is going to go on as if He says, "Now then My dear ones, I can close the parenthesis; I can close the brackets finally. The former things have passed away; now we can get on with the job." We do not know what the job is. All we know is that we are going to be one with Him, joined to Him, the wife of the Lamb, the new Jerusalem, the city of God and God is at home forever there. He is going to manifest His glory. Nations are going to walk in the light of it. I only know there is going to be eternal service. So if you think you are not going to work in heaven you are wrong. There is going to be eternal service. When we come to this matter here, we must ask ourselves: What is the heart of this whole thing? Somewhere we shall understand God's purpose, and I can only say that God's purpose is that you and I should become part of Him.

Partakers of the Divine Nature

That seems almost blasphemous, but note it in the word in II Peter 1:4: "Whereby he hath granted unto us his precious and exceeding great promises; that through these ye may become partakers of the divine nature." So we are to become partakers of the divine nature. We are to become those who are in Christ, those who become the members of Christ. In other words, members mean "part of Christ or limbs of Christ," not members on a church role or on a bit of paper, but members as when we think of a member in the physical body. If the Bible did not say this, it would be almost blasphemous to say that you and I could become part of Christ. Of course, the Lord Jesus never loses His unique deity or His unique position as God the Son. But we become part of Him. How wonderful!

We Christians have done a terrible thing. The gospel we have preached has been so poor that we have given the world the idea that we preach a kind of gospel whereby people get saved, they get forgiven, then they go to church, they sing hymns, they say prayers, they read their Bible every day, and if they are very zealous they witness to others. Then one day they die and sit on a cloud forever playing a harp in an eternal hallelujah chorus. Thus the world turns around and says, "If that is Christianity, you keep it." We have devalued the whole thing. We have made it like a fairy tale. No wonder the new generation says, "What has Christianity got for us?" But that is not Christianity. That is not to devalue the fact of forgiveness or the cost of our forgiveness or justification, but the most glorious thing in the gospel is the fact that God justifies us absolutely, not bit by bit, but absolutely so that our sins and our iniquities He remembers no more.

They are cast away and blotted out; there is not even a record of them. But that is only the beginning; it is a means to an end. When God saved you, it is that you might become a partaker of His nature, that you might become a partner in Him, that you may share His life.

Called into the Fellowship of Jesus Christ Our Lord

1 Corinthians 1:9 says: "God is faithful, through whom you were called into the fellowship of His Son Jesus Christ our Lord." It is not into the fellowship with His Son but into the fellowship of His Son Jesus Christ our Lord.

What is this fellowship of His Son? It is a body. My body is the fellowship of Lance Lambert. You may not like it, but there it is. My little finger says, I am in the fellowship of Lance Lambert." My ears say, "I am in the fellowship of Lance." My foot says I am also in the fellowship of Lance Lambert." My eyes say, "I am in the fellowship of Lance." They are not in your fellowship; you have your own fellowship. Everyone has its own fellowship. Now your fellowship is not sameness, uniformity. You have teeth, ears, eyes, nose, mouth which are all different, but they are in your fellowship.

Now this fellowship is a sharing. My little finger can say, "I have been called into the fellowship of Lance Lambert. I share his life, his intelligence, his mind, his will, and his name. His name is my name." My big toe may say, "I am nowhere near you, little finger. I am right down on the other end, but I share the same life, the same name and the same intelligence when it gets to me down here. I am in the same fellowship." And the apostle Paul says, "God is faithful and you have been called into the fellowship of His Son" (see 1 Corinthians 1:9). We are all members one of another. The eye cannot say to the ear, "I have no need of you." The hand cannot say to the foot, "I have no need of you." We are all in the same fellowship. We belong to each other. We have become sharers of the Lord Jesus Christ.

Koinonia

This Greek word fellowship, koinonia, comes from a word that means "have things in common, to share." In 1 Corinthians 1:9 it says, "God is faithful through whom you have been called into the sharing of His Son Jesus Christ our Lord." My Lord is your Lord. It is very simple. I have a certain racial background, but my Lord is your Lord. You may be a Polynesian, but my Lord is your Lord. In Him there is no Polynesian, no Hebrew, no British, no American. Isn't that marvelous?! You are not American brothers and sisters. You are brothers and sisters from America. I am not a British brother; I am a brother from Britain. There is a great difference. I am a member of the family, not a British member of the family. I am a member of the family who lives in Britain. I am not the church of Richmond, Surry visiting here. I am in the church in Richmond, VA. I am not a visitor; I am a member, so please don't treat me like a visitor. I often used to say to people, "What church did the apostle Paul belong to?" Did he say, "Well, I have my membership in Antioch; I am visiting here to see how you are getting on, then I will go back to Antioch"? Of course not! He was a member of the church of God; he was a member of the family when he went to Ephesus. He became a part of the family in whatever city he visited. The only people who are visitors are the people who are not the Lord's. The rest of us are members of the family.

A Holy Temple to the Lord

What is the purpose of God? Ephesians 2:21: "In whom [the whole building] fitly framed together, groweth into a holy temple in the Lord." Will you please notice it does not say "groweth into a holy temple of the Lord." It says, "It groweth into a holy temple in the Lord." It is a holy temple in the Lord. This changes the whole conception of this matter. If it is a holy temple of the Lord, that is on a lower level from being a holy temple in the Lord. If it is a holy temple of the Lord it means He can visit it. He sort of comes to His temple and says, "Here I am, and I am here to bless you and speak to you. But you are My temple, so I am here for a little while and then good-bye; I am off." Now if we are a holy temple in the Lord then it makes a difference altogether. It means that we are quarried out of the Lord; we are living stones quarried out of the rock of His nature, of His life, out of His substance. We have been produced as living stones and we are being built together in Him. This is wonderful— "in Whom the whole building." In whom? In Christ the whole building fitly framed growth into a holy temple in the Lord.

Builded Together for a Habitation of God

In whom? "In Christ ye also are builded together for a habitation of God in the Spirit" (Ephesians 2:22).That word habitation is an old fashioned word. If you think of the word "dwelling" or better still "home" you have the idea of habitation. It is a home of God in the Spirit in whom ye are buildeth together. In whom? In Christ. It is all in Christ. In Christ the whole building is fitly framed together and grows into a holy temple in the Lord. In Christ we are builded together the home of God in the Spirit.

Somewhere between the first three chapters and the last three chapters we find what the purpose of God is. It is a home for Himself in the Spirit. It is that we might grow into a holy temple in the Lord; that is the purpose of God.

In Ephesians 3:11 it says this: "According to the eternal purpose which he purposed in Christ Jesus our Lord." Or another version puts it: "According to the eternal purpose which he realized in Christ Jesus our Lord." The eternal purpose of God has been realized in Christ Jesus our Lord.

The Tree of Life

This purpose of God which has been realized in Christ Jesus our Lord is all in Him. God has done something in Him. In Genesis 2 we find two things—the tree of life and marriage. The tree of life stands for eternal life. When you eat something, what does it do? It becomes you, so that meal we had a little while earlier is now our flesh and blood. It does not take long. We have the most amazing system in our bodies which turns the meal into flesh and blood within a half hour. Within a matter of an hour or two all this food, which does not look at all like us, is becoming us. So what you eat becomes you. And when you eat of the tree of life, it becomes you. He that eats of Christ and drinks of His blood abideth in Him and He in us. It is life in Him, eternal life. He that eats of Me and drinks of Me, the same shall live because of Me (See John 6). In other words, the Lord Jesus is saying, "He that eats of Us becomes Us, becomes our life, our salvation, our very life." He becomes our strength and power of our being.

Marriage

The second thing we have in Genesis is marriage. When I was first saved, because I had a pagan type of background, when I first began to read the Bible I could never quite understand it and was full of questions. When I first began in Genesis and came to chapter 2, I could not understand why the Lord said to Adam: "Now Adam, you give all these creatures a name." The Lord had created them, why didn't He say, "Now Adam, we will call this a hippopotamus. And this, Adam, is a giraffe and this is an elephant"? But He said to Adam: "You name these things." God was not just interested in Adam naming them. There was something much more in this because the passage begins with this very important statement: "And there was no helpmeet found for him" (see Genesis 2:18, 20). The word in Hebrew is very beautiful; it just means there was not that which answered to his face. There was not anything that answered to him, complemented him, that was him. So God said, "Adam is sinless, he is innocent, but he is not perfect, not complete. So we will bring all these animals before him and see if he finds out by the process that he is missing something." Adam was evidently rather lonely.

So along comes a hippo and Adam says, "I will call that a hippopotamus and off he goes." In comes an elephant, "I will call that an elephant," and off it goes. Here comes a giraffe, and He calls it a giraffe, and off it goes. He does not find anything that answers to him. He may like the creature, he may find it lovable, but he does not find anything that answers to him, even the orangutan when it came before him. Now Adam had never seen another human being, so he might have thought, "Well, I suppose I could settle down with this one. It is the nearest to me and I suppose I am rather lonely. Maybe we could have some sort of relationship that would be mutually helpful." But he said, "No, that is impossible," and the Lord put Adam to sleep. He caused a deep sleep to come upon him. He opened his side and took out of his flesh a bone. Upon the flesh and bone He made woman and then He woke Adam. Did Adam immediately say, "This is woman, good-bye"? No, he said, "This is flesh of my flesh and bone of my bone; this is me. Therefore, the two shall become one."

The Pierced Side of Our Lord Jesus

Our Lord Jesus, the last Adam and the second Man, was put to sleep on the cross, and in John 19:31 He cried, "It is finished!" We know that our salvation was won by that cry, "Finished! Done!" At that moment the veil of the temple was torn in two; it was over. Our salvation was won. Why then does the apostle John make so much of the fact that a Roman soldier pierced the side of Jesus and out of it came blood and water? And the apostle John said, "And he who bears witness with it is true." Why does he make so much of it? When Jesus cried, "It is finished" why didn't John say, "I bore witness and my witness is true"? Isn't that more important. Why did he find the matter of His side being opened and the blood and water coming forth so important? It cannot be salvation because our salvation was already won.

A little later on when John was writing a letter, he said, "There are three that bear witness, the blood, the water and the Spirit." He saw the blood and water as tremendously important. He saw that the Spirit of God would take the blood and water and do something. Of course, what He did was put our Lord Jesus, the last Adam and the second Man to sleep, and His side was opened. And out of His side came blood and water by which a woman is formed, a bride is formed, a church is formed. Then he says, "It is as if the Lord is raised from the dead and comes back and immediately He opens His arms and says, "This is Me." It is a new day, a new creation, a new man, a new beginning. This is Me. You are Me by My finished work through the blood and water from My open side, through the work of the Spirit of God." This is the eternal purpose of God.

When we come to Chronicles, we are not reading some dry dusty old book that just has a few chronicles of some kings thousands and thousands of years ago. It is as if God is saying, "Come with Me; I want you to come behind history. I want to show you what lies behind it all." I want you to understand that all things work together for good to them that love God and who are called according to His purpose. Whether you know it or not you have been called according to purpose. The purpose was not just to save you; the purpose was to make you a home of God which is the calling for which God has called you. He saved you, therefore your salvation is a means to an end. Never make it the end. This is not to devalue your salvation which is so great and so costly, but there is something bigger than even your salvation.

And the thing that is bigger than even your salvation is this glorious end of God which He had in His heart from the beginning to do what He has realized through the finished work of our Lord Jesus Christ and the Spirit.

Looking for a Home

In Genesis 1:2: "The Spirit of God is brooding, hovering..." The word is of an eagle that hovers over darkness, chaos, and emptiness. In the last three chapters, Revelation 22:17 says, "The Spirit and the bride say, 'Come.'" All the way through history it is as if the Spirit of God has been hovering like an eagle looking for a nest, looking for some place where He could alight and find a habitation, but He could not find it. The first time He alights is on one Man, the Lord Jesus at His baptism. The heavens opened and the Spirit of God came down upon Him as a dove. It is as if the Holy Spirit found His home in one Man and now through the finished work of the Lord Jesus Christ, by the blood and the water, the Spirit of God has found His home in a people. And so the Bible ends with these wonderful words: "And the Spirit and the bride say, 'Come.'" It is as if the Holy Spirit is saying, "Here we are, at last I have done it. I have her prepared for her Husband. May the Lord open our eyes, and if we do not understand what I have said may it give us a little appetite. Sometimes it is a good thing to know that there is a good deal more than what we know. May it give us an appetite that we may be like the apostle Paul: "I press on toward the mark for the prize of the high calling of God in Christ Jesus."

2.
The House is Costly

I Chronicles 29:1–9

David the king said unto all the assembly, Solomon my son, whom alone God hath chosen, is yet young and tender, and the work is great; for the palace is not for man, but for the Lord God. Now I have prepared with all my might for the house of my God the gold for the things of gold, and the silver for the things of silver, and the brass for the things of brass, the iron for the things of iron, and wood for the things of wood; onyx stones, and stones to be set, stones for inlaid work, and of divers colors, and all manner of precious stones, and marble stones in abundance. Moreover also, because I have set my affection on the house of my God, seeing that I have a treasure of mine own of gold and silver, I give it unto the house of my God, over and above all that I have prepared for the holy house, even three thousand talents of gold, of the gold of Ophir, and seven thousand talents of refined silver, wherewith to overlay the walls of the houses;

---

*of gold for the things of gold,
and of silver for the things of
silver, and for all manner of
work to be made by the hands
of artificers. Who then offereth
willingly to consecrate himself
this day unto the Lord?*

*Then the princes of the fathers'
houses, and the princes of the
tribes of Israel, and the captains
of thousands and of hundreds,
with the rulers over the king's
work, offered willingly; and they
gave for the service of the house of
God of gold five thousand talents
and ten thousand darics, and
of silver ten thousand talents,
and of brass eighteen thousand
talents, and of iron a hundred
thousand talents. And they
with whom precious stones were
found gave them to the treasure
of the house of the Lord, under
the hand of Jehiel the Gershonite.
Then the people rejoiced, for that
they offered willingly, because
with a perfect heart they offered*

*willingly to the Lord: and David
the king also rejoiced with great joy.*

II Chronicles 1:1–13

*And Solomon the son of
David was strengthened in his
kingdom, and the Lord his God
was with him, and magnified
him exceedingly. And Solomon
spake unto all Israel, to the
captains of thousands and of
hundreds, and to the judges,
and to every prince in all
Israel, the heads of the fathers'
houses. So Solomon, and all the
assembly with him, went to the
high place that was at Gibeon;
for there was the tent of meeting
of God, which Moses the servant
of the Lord had made in the
wilderness. But the ark of God
had David brought up from
Kiriath-jearim to the place that
David had prepared for it; for
he had pitched a tent for it at
Jerusalem. Moreover the brazen
altar, that Bezalel the son of Uri,*

the son of Hur, had made, was there before the tabernacle of the Lord: and Solomon and the assembly sought unto it. And Solomon went up thither to the brazen altar before the Lord, which was at the tent of meeting, and offered a thousand burnt-offerings upon it. In that night did God appear unto Solomon, and said unto him, Ask what I shall give thee. And Solomon said unto God, Thou hast showed great lovingkindness unto David my father, and hast made me king in his stead. Now, O Lord God, let thy promise unto David my father be established; for thou hast made me king over a people like the dust of the earth in multitude. Give me now wisdom and knowledge, that I may go out and come in before this people; for who can judge this thy people, that is so great? And God said to Solomon,

Because this was in thy heart, and thou hast not asked riches, wealth, or honor, nor the life of them that hate thee, neither yet hast asked long life; but hast asked wisdom and knowledge for thyself, that thou mayest judge my people, over whom I have made thee king: wisdom and knowledge is granted unto thee; and I will give thee riches, and wealth, and honor, such as none of the kings have had that have been before thee; neither shall there any after thee have the like. So Solomon came from the high place that was at Gibeon, from before the tent of meeting, unto Jerusalem; and he reigned over Israel.

I would like to say a little more about these two books of Chronicles and what they have to teach us. Chronicles is an interpretation of the whole Old Testament. There are a number of books like that. Deuteronomy is an interpretation of the first four books of the Bible. John is an interpretation of the first three Gospels in the New Testament. Chronicles goes right behind all history from Adam to the return from Babylon; indeed, you could say from Adam to the coming of the Lord Jesus tells us the secret of God's purpose.

The Key to Chronicles

If you will carefully go through Chronicles, reading it either in a very modern colloquial version or in an older version, you will discover that the reign of every king of Judah is judged by their attitude to the house of God. Now we know from archeology that some of these kings were great kings, but you would not learn that from the Bible. Some of them are just given a few verses and dismissed, but in fact they were very great kings with times of great prosperity outwardly and of great building programs. But the scriptures bypass them and overlooks them because of their attitude to the house of the God. In other words, if you and I had been there we would have written history differently. We would have said, "Now this man is a big man who has a really big name for a great organization. He has everything at his fingertips; but God says, "No. He is nothing. That is all just transient; it just belongs to time. It was all show; it was all flesh; it was all human resources and does not go into the city of God. However, the king who had a difficult time did something as far as the house of God was concerned. So we have quite a lot about Hezekiah, Josiah, Jehoshaphat, and other such kings.

We have therefore seen that the key to these two books of Chronicles is the house of God, the dwelling place of God, a home for God. This is something God has been after all through the ages, right behind history and right behind the creation of man. It lies behind God's redeeming purpose, His saving purpose. He has saved you with a very great objective in view—not just that you might be forgiven, not just that you may be filled with the Spirit, but that you might be built together for a habitation of God in the Spirit. You may become the home of God for all eternity, the place where God is at home, the place where God reveals Himself, the place where God manifests Himself, the place from which God rules and reigns, the place where all the beauty of the character of the Lord God is to be forever expressed. That is God's plan for you, and that is a high calling. That is no small, mean thing. That is something tremendous. When you think that we are such worthless, insignificant, sinful creatures, how more amazing is the grace of God! How amazing is the grace of God, not only to forgive and justify us, and to declare that we are righteous, but it is to bring us into this relationship with Himself for all eternity.

There are a number of things I would like to underline from these two books of Chronicles. And the first thing I would like to underline is that the sovereign purpose and power of God are behind this building. In other words, God's sovereignty, His all-mightiness, His omnipotence, His infinite power were thrown behind this plan to get this house of God built, and that is why when we look into Chronicles we find that there is behind all history a mighty flow of God's power and might. The pedigrees and genealogies we talked about in the first ten chapters of I Chronicles, which many people find so terribly boring, are just an illustration of this. There are all kinds of people in those genealogies and lots of them go out of the purpose of God. They had a relationship with God, but as far as the purpose of God is concerned they go out.

The Sovereignty of God

Marxists speak about the inexorable march of human history. They speak about this sort of "onward march" of some sort of impersonal thing called history. But we believers have something far more wonderful. There is flowing from God sovereign power, and God has a purpose which He is not going to be frustrated over. Come wind, come weather, even if all hell comes out against God, He is not going to be frustrated in this purpose. He had this in His heart from the beginning. What was it? To provide a bride for His Son, to produce a home for Himself in the Spirit. Satan seemed to come in and destroy and frustrate that, but he has not. He has only made the grace of God the more wonderful because God sent His own Son, the very One for whom we were destined in the beginning, to lay down His life to bring us back to Himself. So God has not been frustrated but through His Son has given us a salvation by which His original purpose for us can be fulfilled. That is marvelous, isn't it? It is a tremendous panorama of our salvation and makes us realize that salvation is not just some "thing." Behind it lies this inexorable onward march of the sovereignty of God. He is not going to be frustrated.

I cannot understand these people who tell me that the church is in ruins and it is all sort of hopeless, all fragmented, all divided, all in pieces, and now all we have to do is go on personally with the Lord. The Lord Jesus said in Matthew 16:18: "Upon this rock I will build my church." And just to make absolutely sure that no one can misunderstand the Lord, He said, "And the gates of hell shall not prevail against it." Who are these Christians who tell us that the gates of hell have prevailed against it? What do they mean? Are you going to side with the devil in this matter? There are plenty of Christians who are just propaganda machines for the devil. They say, "It cannot be done. It is all mystical, idealistic. This matter of our being built together, about our really coming together and knowing the oneness of the Lord Jesus Christ, knowing something of what it is to go on with Him, to grow up into Him as the Head, is all mystical. Be careful of it; it is idealistic stuff."

The Lord Jesus said, "Thou art Peter," and there was no one who was more shaky than Peter. There was no one who was more impetuous and impulsive than Peter. He was always putting his foot in it. As we say in Ireland, "He is always opening his mouth and putting his foot in it." Peter was always in the front, but he did not have at that time the stability, power and roots to go through. It was more on the surface; it was the flesh; it was his own resources. Peter is just like us all. If the Lord had said, "Thou art John and upon this rock I will build," we would have understood a lot more. We would have said, "That cuts a lot of us out. We do not have that devotion to the Lord. We do not have that intimate leaning upon His breast that he had." But the Lord chose Peter who, after all, is like us all. He loved His Lord, but he said things quickly and thought about it afterwards. He was always in the front line, always taking the lead. It was not just ambition; he really loved his Lord and he wanted to be wholly with Him. Oh, how lovely that the Lord said, "Thou art Peter, just a little splinter of the Rock, and upon this rock, the great Massif, I will build My church, and the gates of hell shall not prevail against it."

What does Chronicles teach us? If we take Ezra and Nehemiah in with it too, it teaches us that even in spite of all hell, God's purpose is going to be fulfilled. Even if the people of God are sent into Babylon and dispersed into every part of the earth, yet still the purpose of God will be fulfilled, if only in a handful. If God has to raise up children from the stones He will do it. Don't think that God is sort of perplexed. He is not perplexed at all.

If the Lord cannot get His way with us He will get it with someone else. He will raise up, if He needs to, a new generation altogether that has nothing to do with this. Why He might even do something in Jewish circles altogether apart from Christendom that will finally give Him His purpose and plan in the end; but He is going to do it. Our Lord Jesus has committed Himself. He said, "Upon this rock I will build My church and the gates of hell shall not prevail against it."

The Mystery of God's Will

I often hear people say, "I wish I knew the will of God for me." Listen, you will always be in a mess when you take this in a self-centered way. "What is the will of God for me? What should I do?

What should my career be? Where should I live? How should I go?" First of all get the stick round the other way, sort of turn the whole thing, invert the order. First, get hold of what is God's will. What is God's will? Then a whole lot of things will fall into place once you begin to see what God's will is, once you begin to see what His will is for His people, what is really behind all history. This will give you a clarity that you have never had before in your life. We are all so self-centered. We believe the Lord revolves around us. He is there for me. The throne of God is for me, just a clearer way for me to live this life. Salvation, of course, is for me. Everything is for me. I am the center of the world. The Lord is there for me, the Father is there for me, even the Holy Spirit is there for me, and everyone else is there for me. I am the center of it all. Get rid of that idea. It is the Lord who is the center and you are revolving around Him. Go over onto the other side; begin to see it like that.

There are lots of scriptures about this. It says in Ephesians 1:9–10: "Making known unto us the mystery of his will, according to his good pleasure which he purposed in him [Christ] unto a dispensation of the fullness of the times, to sum up all things in Christ."

Here is the will of God. Here is the mystery of His will and He has made it known to us. What is this mystery of His will? To sum up all things in Christ. Christ everything and in everyone—Christ all and in all. This is the purpose of God.

We do know that the will of God for us is always along the line that we must decrease and He must increase. There must be more and more of Him. So that is one way we can always find out whether it is the will of God for us. Does it glorify me? Does it satisfy me only? Or is it really the Lord that is getting something out of this?

Colossians 1:9–10: "For this cause we also, since the day we heard it, do not cease to pray and make request for you, that ye may be filled with the knowledge of his will in all spiritual wisdom and understanding, to walk worthily of the Lord unto all pleasing, bearing fruit in every good work, and increasing in the knowledge of God."

There is nothing more wonderful than to be in the center of the will of God. I do not just mean you personally in detail, but to be in the center of God's will concerning this home for Himself in the Spirit. When you get there, surely everything else will start to fall into place because there you are right in the center of the main tide of the purpose of God which has not changed through all history. I find it the most thrilling thing in the world. I cannot understand Christians who get all tied up and weighed down. Look at me; I am just a little tiny human being, a little bit of clay, flesh and blood, a dot amongst the billions and billions of human beings, not only who are alive but have ever lived. And little me, by the grace of God, can get right into the center of the flow of the purpose of God from eternity to eternity. I can feel a great current that takes me forward.

Being in the Flow of the Current of the Spirit of God

Once when we flew from San Francisco home to London, we flew in a 707 and were told by the pilot that they had just begun that flight. It was the extent of what the 707 could do without coming down to refuel, and they told us why it could do this. We can do this because we get into the slip stream. We get into a flow of warm air which rushes up to the arctic and it carries us right the way up and then we put the engine in full blast and it comes down to London. Now I am not a technical person so those of you who are forgive me if I put it rather crudely. But the fact of the matter is that little plane got into a mighty current of air and it just swept us along. You may not get into a current of air, but you can get into the current of the Spirit of God. You can get into the flow of the divine life of God. You can get into the sovereign power and might of God Himself which will carry you through because God has a great purpose and you will be in it.

How Will the Building Be Completed?

You remember what Zechariah said in chapter 4 when he saw the vision of the olive trees and the lampstand all of gold? He asked what it was all about and the angel said to him: "Not by might, nor by power, but by my Spirit, saith the Lord of hosts. Who art thou, O great mountain? Before Zerubbabel thou shalt become a plain; and he shall bring forth the top stone with shoutings of Grace, grace, unto it" (vv. 6b–7).

Now some of you who have real charismatic experience, surely you think it will not be shouts of grace but glory, glory, unto it. But no, there will be such difficulties, such problems that will make the whole thing impossible by human standards. It will be only by the Spirit through faith, and when it is done the only thing we will be able to cry is "grace"; the grace of God has completed the work. He laid the foundation; He developed the building; He brought the top stone, which is the Messiah, into place. It is all His work. Oh how wonderful it is to be in this building! I do not care where I am. I do not care whether I am a little stone somewhere in some corner buried out of sight or whether I am a bigger stone somewhere else or whether I am in an arch. I do not care where I am as long as I am in the building. I want to be somewhere between the foundation and the top stone. That is all. When I am between the foundation and the top stone, glory be to God, I am in the purpose of God. I am in the heart of the yearning of God's heart from eternity to eternity. I am right where He wants me to be as far as the salvation of His Son. It is not just to save me and make me a pretty little object; it is to bring me into something that is going to be forever and ever and ever the instrument of the purposes of God. We do not know what they are, but how wonderful it is to be a part of it. We have such a high calling; why drop out?

Do not be a Dropout

These pedigrees, these genealogies in the first ten chapters are all about people who dropped out. Many of them were really connected with the purpose of God. For instance, Adam, he went right out. And Esau, he went right out. There was Saul and many others who went out. They are all listed here. There is an extraordinary little comment inserted in these pedigrees. It says of one person: "He trusted the Lord and did valiantly." Why is that in the pedigrees? Because it meant something to the Lord. That man had great problems and we do not know who he is or anything about him, but he is inserted there and did valiantly because he trusted in the Lord. A lot of people just went out. It says of Saul that he went out because he inquired of a medium. He compromised, he touched another world, the enemy of God, and he went out. Don't drop out. There are plenty of dropouts in the world, but there are also plenty of spiritual dropouts. They become Christian cynics. They get so disillusioned and disappointed by everything and everybody they just become cynics. They become critics or Christian agnostics. Outwardly they believe everything; inwardly they believe nothing. There are plenty of them. They do not really believe anything and yet they are frightened to say that they do not believe. God preserve us from being dropouts. May we be in the purpose of God right through to the end.

If this house of God is going to be built there is a need for a deep and costly preparation. We have it all here in Chronicles. One thing that we find in I Chronicles 11:4–9 is that David had to take Jerusalem. There could be no building of this house of God until Jerusalem was taken, and Jerusalem was a Jebusite city. Now the Lord had said, "Every place where the sole of your foot treads upon, that will I give you." He had said that to Moses and to Joshua. And wherever they put the sole of their feet down and said, "This is ours!" it happened. Through faith then there was a real preparation.

If you want to be in this building, if you want to be builded together for a home of God in the Spirit, if you want to contribute something towards its building, let me tell you it will ever and only be by grace through faith. It is never any other way. It was all grace that God said, "I will send the angel of My presence before you and he will be like a hornet. He will drive out all the "ites." All will be driven out and you shall possess the land. It was grace, but then comes your responsibility of faith. Wheresoever the soles of your feet tread upon that will I give you. You have to put the soles of your feet somewhere, and that is what they did.

Put the Soles of Your Feet Down

You remember the River Jordan? It was overflowing in the full harvest time. I always think the Lord has humor. If only He had allowed it to be in the dry season where the river was a little smaller and the priests could have just gone down and said, "Well, we cannot get across this, but it does not look too bad. Maybe it will dry up a bit more and we will be able to wade across somehow or other." But no it was full harvest time. And don't you think, as those priests took the ark of the covenant down to the water, the devil was right there whispering in their ears: "You are going to look like a bunch of fools in the sight of these people. All you are going to do is get your feet wet. You are going to stand in the water there and not a thing is going to happen." And don't you think one of them might have thought: "Now Lord, give us a sign. As we move down, let the waters go back just a little, then we will know You are with us."

I know many people like this who say, "Lord, I cannot take this step of faith until You give me a sign. Just let the water go back a little." But if I know the Lord He will let the water come out and meet you. A great high wave will come at you as much as to say, "Ha, Ha, you are not going to get across." But the priests of the

Lord just put their feet down into the water onto the river bed, and as soon as the soles of their feet touched the river bed the water stopped.

Of course, there are people who think that the thing they must do, they have to do it quickly. They say, "Now then just put the soles of your feet down and say, 'Lord, I take this; now come on. Do it, do it.'" And if it does not happen instantly, they say, "The Lord is not with us; what is wrong? There must be sin in the camp or something else."

The Walls of Jericho

When they came to Jericho they had to go round once a day for six days and on the seventh day seven times. And the masterly thing of the Lord was that there was not to be a single bit of conversation. Have you ever found that when you take a step in faith, conversation is not always a good thing? People will come and say, "Do you really think? I wonder. I am not sure." On the other hand, conversation is a good thing. What do you think those people in Jericho must have thought as they looked over the walls and saw this great crowd of people going round? They think: "What are they, tourists from Egypt? Look at them just going round the wall." One old divine once said, "There are only two ways of looking at those walls. One was, 'Poof, these walls? They will never come down.' Or the other one is: 'What a lot of dust there will be when these walls come down.'"

But on the seventh day on the seventh time when the trumpet of the Lord blew and they shouted with a great shout, the walls fell flat. They had used the soles of their feet. It was grace by faith. Those children of God were judged all the way through by what they took or what they did not take. In some places they found chariots of iron, and they said it is too hard. What a tragedy! They only needed to use the soles of their feet. They did not have to battle with chariots of iron. They just had to put their feet down on that valley and say, "Chariots of iron or no chariots of iron, this is the Lord's valley!" And it would have been the Lord's valley, but they said, "There are chariots of iron."

There are many Christians who have known many great deliverances and many great victories, but when they come to the chariots of iron, they take one look at those rumbling chariots, like the tanks of our day, and say, "No, no, no! This is no good; this is a bit too much."

When they came to Jerusalem, they said, "Jerusalem! Impossible!" And for four hundred years Jerusalem remained a Jebusite city until David came and used the soles of his feet, and Jerusalem was taken—and it became Jerusalem.

If you and I are going to know anything about building, the first thing that has to be taken is Jerusalem—not just the land. It is not just that you must enter into the fullness of Christ, you have got to take a particular place in the land which the enemy will do every single thing to stop you from taking. What is that? It is the purpose of God to have a home for Himself in the Spirit. In other words, it is our being built together in a particular place at a particular time. You have got to take it. If you do not take Jerusalem you will be out. You will know something of the fullness of Christ, but you will not be in the central stream of the purpose of God.

The Building Materials

Then I want to say something else about this need for deep and costly preparation. All this gold, this silver, this brass, this iron, these precious stones, this wood, were nearly all the spoils of victories. However small your victory is, it yields spoil. You have a big problem. Maybe it is a problem about worldliness and you have had such a battle over this thing. You love this thing which was the very essence of your life before you were saved. Then you got saved and suddenly you feel uncovered. It is not other people who have talked to you about it, but the Holy Spirit has been dealing with you about that particular issue, and for you it is huge. Others think it is nothing. So you say, "What does it matter? If I do get through, what does it matter? Who is going to gain from this? Is anyone going to gain from it?" When you get through, there is spoil for the house of the Lord. There is gold that comes into your life, the gold of His nature that can come no other way. There is silver that comes into your life, something more of His redeeming work. There is brass that comes into your life, something of His power, iron that comes into your life. All these things come into your life through victories.

In 1 Chronicles 20:2b it says, "And he brought forth the spoil of the city, exceeding much."

Chapter 26:26–27: "This Shelomoth and his brethren were over all the treasures of the dedicated things, which David the king, and the heads of the fathers' houses, the captains over thousands and hundreds, and captains of the host, had dedicated. Out of the spoil won in battles did they dedicate to repair the house of the Lord."

There is such a battle for life if you are a child of God. And if you know anything of fellowship with one another in a growing way, what a battle that is! It is as if all hell is out to fragment us, divide us, to somehow trip us up and ensnare us, but every time we know a victory of the Lord by grace through faith then there is spoil for the house of the Lord. There is gold, silver, brass, iron, precious stones, and all of these are qualities of Christ. How do they come into our lives? They come at great cost. They do not just come as you sit there and do nothing.

Don't Wait Until You are Perfect Before You Function

Some people feel that until they are spiritual they can do nothing, but you will sit there until kingdom come and not be one whit more spiritual. So continue sitting. If you really think: "I cannot take part; I could never praise the Lord in a company like this, I cannot open my mouth and pray, not until I am more spiritual. I will leave that to the more spiritual." You will never be more spiritual till you open your mouth and praise the Lord in the midst of the people of God. You will never ever know anything more of the Lord until you take a step in faith. Behind it all lies pride. Some of us will not speak another language till we are perfect, so we never learn it. You say, "I am not going to open my mouth and make a fool of myself." You will never get anywhere. You will never walk unless you learn to fall. When you learn to stumble and you are picked up and go on, or you fall and someone helps you get up, after a while you start getting up yourself and before long you are walking. We have to learn these deep lessons.

We have to get victories in these things. They may seem very small, but very big things depend on victories in small issues. Never forget that. The devil will tell you that it is something very small and does not mean anything; it is a lie. That thing may be very small in itself but once you settle it you will find that the gateway opens to a huge universe of spiritual wealth and it will all be yours increasingly. The spoils of victory over the enemies of God go into the building of this house.

Gold Refined in the Fire

Again I want to say it is very costly sacrifice. These things do not just come. You read in 1 Chronicles 22:14: "Now, behold, in my affliction I have prepared for the house of the Lord." "In my affliction"—David knew pretty well about afflictions. There was much in his life that can only be described as affliction. Years and years of being hounded in the wilderness by Saul. He could have polished Saul off two or three times but he refused to do so because he would not allow the arm of flesh to help the work of God. And that meant more affliction for him. There are times when the Lord tries us. He says, "Here you are, you can polish this thing off, just do it now. If you just take this action you will finish it and you will be on the throne." But to do that would be to introduce another level, another realm into the work of God, the realm of the flesh. When you say "no", you introduce yourself to much more affliction. But you see there is a sacrifice in this whole matter. Do you really think that gold comes easily? Jesus said to the church at Laodicea which thought it was so rich, so great, so powerful and needed nothing, "I counsel thee to buy of Me gold refined in the fire." Why did He say, "I counsel Thee to buy of Me"? How can you buy something which is given to you by grace? I believe the cost is experience. It is by grace that the gold comes to you, but experience is the price. And sometimes you must go into death before, by the grace of God, you know that gold given to you.

Treasure in Earthen Vessels

Oh, there are many other ways. For instance, in II Corinthians 4:7–10 the apostle Paul says, "But we have this treasure in earthen vessels, that the exceeding greatness of the power may be of God, and not from ourselves; we are pressed on every side, yet not straitened; perplexed, yet not unto despair; pursued, yet not forsaken; smitten down, yet not destroyed; always bearing about in the body the dying of Jesus, that the life also of Jesus may be manifested in our body."

Here is an experience. We would say, "A Christian perplexed? No Christian ought to be perplexed." We would say, "Indeed! An apostle perplexed? We do not have apostles to be perplexed. We have apostles to be clear! We have leaders to be clear! If they are not clear, how can we be clear?" The apostle says, "perplexed, always perplexed, yet not unto despair." You see there is some affliction there. It does not mean he is not clear about the Lord. He may be very clear about the Lord, the ways of the Lord, and the purpose of the Lord, but he is greatly perplexed at times. And the Lord allows it. Why? Because there is treasure in that vessel and the only way to get the treasure out is to break the vessel, and the only way to break a vessel is by being pressed on every side, perplexed, pursued, smitten down, bearing about in the body the dying of Jesus. It is the only way your treasure can come out. If Christ is in you there is treasure in there, unsearchable riches of Christ, but how to get them out? "For our light affliction, which is for the moment, worketh for us more and more exceedingly an eternal weight of glory" (v. 17). This light affliction is employed by God to bring about and produce an eternal weight of glory. There is a need for deep and costly preparation if you and I would be part of this building.

The Unswerving Purpose of Heart

One other thing in this matter I would like to mention. There must be an unswerving purpose of heart. No man or woman will ever be prepared to pay the price of being in this building work of God unless they have an unswerving purpose of heart. Or to put it another way, a single eye for the Lord. If you are double-minded, if there are two ways about you, you will go out in the end. You will be a dropout. Get that double mind dealt with by God if you have got one. Get that serving of God and mammon dealt with by God if you are trying to do it. It will destroy you; it will surely destroy you! You will be a drop out as far as the purpose of God goes.

David Saw the House of God

In rabbinical circles Psalm 23 is attributed to David's youth when he was a shepherd lad. How amazing that a boy could write a Psalm like this, if that is true: "The Lord is my shepherd, I shall not want. He makes me to lie down." And the most remarkable thing is this: "Surely goodness and mercy shall follow me all the days of my life, and I will dwell in the house of the Lord forever." What is this little lad talking about? Where did he get this from? House of the Lord? Where is the house of the Lord? There was no house of the Lord. What is this boy talking about? "And I will dwell in the house of the Lord." He was a shepherd boy. He knew all about killing bears and lions, keeping the flock from foes, but what did he know about the house of God? The rabbis used to say that Jesse, the father of David, was by trade a weaver of the veil of the tabernacle. If that is true, then it may be that the dear old father of David's used to say, "It is about time we had a real place for this veil. That old tent has really served its purpose." I do not know but somewhere in the youth of David by the Spirit of God he claimed to see the house of God. Later on he said in Psalm 27:4: "One thing have I asked of the Lord, that will I seek after: that I may dwell in the house of the Lord all the days of my life, to behold the beauty of the Lord, and to inquire in his temple."

What a purpose this man had. It was unswerving. He would not be diverted one way or the other. He had many failings and faults, but David had an unswerving purpose and by the grace of God David was not a dropout. He was within the purpose of God right through to the end. That is why that lovely Psalm 132 was written about David: "Lord, remember for David all his affliction; how he sware unto the Lord, and vowed unto the Mighty One of Jacob: surely I will not come into the tabernacle of my house, nor go up into my bed; I will not give sleep to mine eyes, or slumber to mine eyelids; until I find out a place for the Lord, a tabernacle for the Mighty One of Jacob" (vv. 1–5). There is purpose.

When the Tabernacle and Ark Get Parted

I just want to touch on this in II Chronicles 1:3, and here you will see that the tabernacle and ark had gotten parted. The tent of meeting of God was at Gibeon and the ark of the Lord was in Jerusalem. They had gotten parted. Now the ark of the Lord stands for the presence of the Lord, the committed presence of the Lord. The presence of the Lord, of course, is everywhere, but this is the committed presence of the Lord. And the symbol of the committed presence of the Lord was the ark. Of course, we see it most beautifully in our Lord Jesus in whom there is both authority—Aaron's rod that budded—and the golden pot of manna—He is the bread of life—and the unbroken law—the law fulfilled. Of course, He is also the mercy seat. The fact is that the ark was the symbol of the committed presence of God. "The Word became flesh and dwelt among us. We beheld His glory, glory as of the only begotten of the Father, full of grace and truth."

Somehow the presence of the Lord and the tent of meeting, which is a symbol of us in Christ, a symbol of our being in Him and together with Him, has gotten parted. All through church history the ark of the Lord and the tent of meeting have been getting parted. All through church history right from the beginning the devil has worked unceasingly to divorce the ark of the Lord from the tent of meeting. And then comes the division amongst the people of God: "Where should we go? What should we do? Shall we serve the Lord in the tent of meeting? Shall we serve the Lord at the ark of God?" When the ark and the tent of meeting get parted, always follow the ark. In other words, it is best and safest to follow the Lord than to follow just the outward organization or system.

When God does this building, the tent of meeting has to come to the ark, not the ark to the tent of meeting. What is this cry that is going up all the time: "We need revival; we need revival!"? Is it not so often that we want the ark of the Lord to come to our tent of meeting? It is our work we want revived, our denomination we want revived, our circle we want revived. It is not that God does not want to revive His people, but the only way it can happen is by bringing the circle to the ark of the Lord. This may require quite a few changes. Some people want revival without any changes. They just want it to go straight into the old ruts and fill it, just somehow or other get into the old thing and give it a bit of light, bring in a few more members, increase the collections and generally help. I know it sounds very unkind, but believe me I have not been in the Lord's work for nothing. I have had ministers sometimes say to me: "You know, we can hardly make it now because our congregations are dropping, the collections are poor, and all the rest of it; we need revival." That may seem very unkind but it is the truth. But for the grace of God all of us would naturally think on that level. "We need to see the place filled if we are going to go on!" Those folks really believe there is a testimony of the Lord in this thing, but God says, "No, I do not take the ark to the tent, the tent must come to the ark." You see, many changes may be required. The ark has not gone wrong; it is the tent. Bring the tent to the ark; in other words, bring the holy vessels of God back.

It was not the tent of meeting that actually went to the ark in the end; it was all the holy vessels that were taken to it. I have just mentioned it because many of us want God's revival or renewal or however you want to put it on our terms.

Let me tell you a true story. In the West of England in a quite hilly area called North Devon there is much wild open country called Exmore. There are two beautiful resorts; Lynton and Lynmouth. Lynmouth is on the mouth of the river and Lynton is up on the top of the cliffs. Quite a few years ago, about 1952, there were three days of torrential rain up on the moors and the water built up and built up and built up, till finally a huge wall of water sixty feet high crashed down upon the sleeping resort of Lynmouth. It carried away two-thirds of the town into the sea. Cars were taken over one hundred miles into the Irish Sea and many, many people lost their lives. Many were never found again including believers.

When an inquiry was held, it was found that the course of the river Lyn had been changed by man. Sixty or seventy years before they had changed the course of the river Lyn and had given it a new course, and when the flood came, the river went back to its old course. Every time that God has visited His people in the history of the church, the tide of life has gone back to the old course, the primitive course, the New Testament course. We changed it! We do not like the river going this way; we like it to come this way—much prettier, more convenient, and so we built a new way for the river. But when the tide of God's blessing comes, really comes, back God goes to the old. He says, "No, you come back to Me, I do not come to you.

The Need for Vision in the Building of the House

There are two other things I want to touch on in this book of Chronicles. One is the need of vision. Is there anything more beautiful in the book of Chronicles than this picture of the young Solomon offering up one thousand offerings on the brazen altar and then he goes off to bed? And in the night the Lord stood by him in a vision and said, "Ask what I shall give thee." Has God ever asked you a question? Sometimes God asks you a question through the lips of another human being, and you do not even realize it is the Lord that is asking you the question. Shall I tell you something? We often give the game away by our answer. You reveal very much about yourself in the way you answer a question. If we are going to see anything about building the first thing we must have is vision.

The Pattern for the Church

The church has suffered from people who have studied church doctrine and tried to put it into practice. Oh, how the world is cluttered with New Testament patterns all over the place. Here is a New Testament pattern; there is a New Testament pattern, over there is a New Testament pattern. They all have a New Testament pattern which is built upon Scripture. And sometimes we find these New Testament patterns are more deadly than something which is definitely not a New Testament pattern. Sometimes we find in some circles, which we cannot by any stretch of the imagination call a New Testament church in practice, there is more of the presence of the Lord, more blessing and more life. On the other hand, if we go to one of these New Testament churches, it is as cold as a graveyard; it is as cold as death. What is the problem? Surely we have a New Testament pattern, and if we have a New Testament pattern, surely the Lord should be committed to it. Surely once you have a New Testament pattern, once you have the regulations, once you have the pattern, once you have got everything according to Scripture, the Lord should be delighted, absolutely falling over Himself to bless them all and be with them and use them! Not at all. The Lord has a horror of New Testament patterns, unless it is the pattern that comes from within His life.

My body has a pattern—two eyes, two ears, a nose, a mouth, two hands, two legs. I have a pattern and so have you, but my pattern was not put together by a book. My mother did not read a book and say, "Now then, you have got to be like this, do not forget! You have two legs, two hands, two eyes, two ears, and a nose. You must be like that." Not at all. All my mother did was eat the right food and get the right rest and I came along. I have the pattern inside and it is in the life.

The Onions and a Daffodil

If I were to plow up a large field of three or four acres and plant thousands and thousands of onions and in the center was one daffodil, do you know that all those onions would come up as onions and the one daffodil would still be a daffodil? But you would say, "That is extraordinary; the bulbs look so much alike." Recently we had a man in England who was in the hospital from eating daffodil bulbs. His wife had had some daffodils flowering indoors and had taken them out and put them near the vegetables. While his wife was a little unwell he went out and took what he thought were onions, shredded them and had a good meal because he could not tell the difference between the daffodil bulbs and onion bulbs.

Wouldn't you think that thousands and thousands of onion bulbs being so near one little daffodil would make it an onion? All those thousands and thousands of onions, with all their fellowship, their influence, and their nearness together surely ought to make one little daffodil like them. He ought to be able to say, "I feel a bit lonely and I look so like them, I will be an onion too." But he cannot do it. He has daffodil life and the rest have onion life. So the onions come up onions and the daffodil comes up a daffodil. It is the life, and there is a pattern in the life. You have to see this.

This whole thing began when Solomon saw God standing by him. Isaiah's ministry also began when he was in the temple and he saw the Lord high and lifted up with His train filling the temple. He was evidently bowing, I suppose, in prayer, lifting up his hands to God, and then all of a sudden he looked and he thought, "What has happened? It is like a fog everywhere. I cannot see the temple anymore." Then he looked at it more carefully and his eyes began to go up and up and up and he saw the Lord high and lifted up. The Lord enveloped the whole temple. The temple was lost in the Lord, and Isaiah could no longer see it. Some people only see the church, and that is the whole problem. But when we see the church as the Lord, oh that is different! We see the church as being in Christ. We see the church as the life of Christ being expressed. It makes all the difference in the world. If you want to see God do something in the way of building wherever you live it must begin with vision. Start asking the Lord for vision. May He give you the spirit of wisdom and revelation in the knowledge of the Lord, the eyes of your hearts being enlightened that you may know—not about—but you may know. May God grant this.

Dividing of Soul and Spirit

Then I want to note the order. First, Solomon offered a thousand burnt offerings on the altar and then received the vision. Many people strain and stress, really striving to get a vision: "I want to see this thing; I want to see this thing." God does not show anything lightly to people. First, He demands that you know something of the cross in your life. One thousand burnt offerings is no small burnt offering. That was something total, something absolute. Have you yet come to an experience of the cross? Do you know what it is to lay down your life? Do you know what it is to be identified with the Lord Jesus Christ in His death, burial and resurrection? Do you know anything about that at all? About bearing in your body the dying of Jesus that the life may also be manifested? I tell you, vision comes out of that. There has to be a cleavage between soul and spirit if we are to see.

The Need for Wisdom in the Building of the House

And then there is the need for wisdom. I said a moment ago the answer to a question says a lot about you. God came to Solomon and said, "Ask Me what I shall give you." I would be so interested if the Lord spoke to every one of us. It would not be a collective thing; He would not say, "Ask what I shall give you all." He would come to each one of us quietly, standing before us and simply say, with no long revelation or long message, one short direct question: "Ask what I shall give you?" I would love to know what you would ask. That would be the surest indication of the kind of person you are. Supposing the Lord stood in front of you just now, and there is nobody else in this room and said: "Tell Me what I should give you; what would you like? What is your supreme want and need?"

Solomon Asked for Wisdom

Solomon could have asked for power, for security, for popularity, for riches, for the death of his enemies, for help, for long life; he asked for none of these. In many ways many of these things would have been quite legitimate—power that I might reign, riches that I not fall into poverty, security that I might give myself to knowing how to rule this people, the death of my enemies, (he was twenty-one years of age and had the most hard and cruel and cunning enemies. Joab was one and there were others all around this young man who were ready to assassinate him, ready to do anything to get rid of him). He could have asked: "Fetter my enemies, Lord, because they are Your enemies." He could have asked for health because I am not a healthy person." He asked for one thing—wisdom.

I must say that I think this is the forgotten quality. I hardly ever hear people asking for wisdom. I just do not hear people asking for wisdom; not even people who are responsible in the work of God. I do not hear them asking for wisdom. They ask for power, they ask for fullness and that is not wrong, but listen to what the Lord said. He fell over Himself almost to say, "Solomon! Because you asked for this thing not for yourself but that you might rule this people for Me, I will give you all the things you did not ask for. You shall have everything because you asked for this. I will give you wisdom such as no one has ever had before or after you. And then I will give you all the power, fullness, riches, wealth, the death of your enemies, health and long life. I will give them all to you because you have asked for wisdom." That is the value that God puts on wisdom above everything else.

The Fear of the Lord is the Beginning of Wisdom

The Scripture is very interesting in this way. In Proverbs 4:7, it says: "Wisdom is the principle thing, therefore get wisdom, yea with all thy getting, get understanding." Wisdom is the principle thing, therefore get wisdom.

Or again in chapter 9:10: "The fear of the Lord is the beginning of wisdom; and the knowledge of the Holy One is understanding." Oh, where is this fear of the Lord? This is the one thing Solomon had: he feared the Lord and that is why he asked for wisdom. For the fear of the Lord is the beginning of wisdom.

And this fear of the Lord is not some cringing thing that depraves you or robs you of dignity. This fear is the loving, sensitive reverence and affection for the Lord that you would not dare to do anything that would upset Him or grieve Him. Oh, how we need wisdom.

Many years ago when I was a lad and newly saved, I did not know a single thing about the Bible or anything to do with Christian things at all. Around the corner from us in a huge mansion lived a Swedish lady that I knew as Auntie Dagmar. She was a dear believer and she took me and my sister under her wing. And some of the first lessons we ever learned from her were the deepest and lasted all the way through the years. I remember she said to me once, "Now my boy, you ask the Lord for wisdom and you ask Him every morning and every night." And she gave me a scripture which was James 1:5–6a: "But if any of you lacketh wisdom, let him ask of God, who giveth to all liberally and upbraideth not; and it shall be given him. But let him ask it faith, nothing wavering." I used to pray every morning and every night religiously for wisdom, quoting that scripture. I am so glad that I did, and I still do. I have found again and again that when we ask the Lord for wisdom, in the most wonderful way, not in a dramatic way, but in the most wonderful way, the treasures of knowledge and wisdom which are hidden in our Lord Jesus Christ are made available to us.

It is interesting that in 1 Corinthians 1:30 it says, "But of him are ye in Christ Jesus, who was made unto us wisdom ..." and then it goes on. But the first thing that He is made to us is wisdom. Do we put enough value on wisdom? I do not believe the house of God will ever be built until we see this.

Wisdom vs. Knowledge

I will close by telling you a story. What is the difference between wisdom and knowledge? Do you know the difference between wisdom and knowledge? I will tell you the difference by illustrating it. Behind Halford house we have what you call a truck farm; we call it the market garden. The old man who farmed that area, about two acres, was a man called Dan Archer. He was an absolute character. This man became the basis for a whole series on BBC which has run now for sixteen years. Every day there is fifteen minutes of The Archers. He is gone now, he died some years ago.

We had a beautiful fuchsia bush which had been at Halford House for years and years. Halford House dates to 1710, but the fuchsia was not that old. It was a thing of great beauty when it was in bloom. This one year when it came out, it had all the leaves and buds, but just as the buds were about to open they all fell off. Then there were more buds and just when they were about to open they all fell. We could not understand it. Now we had two of the leading botanists in the British Commonwealth in the company in Halford House in Richmond. So we went to them and I said, "Could you please explain what is wrong with the fuchsia." So independently, they both came, and they were very interesting. They plucked off the leaves and looked up at the sky through them, they looked very carefully at the bark, they inspected the bloom, and then they said, "Well, it could be this." And they mentioned a Latin name. "Or it could be that or it is probably this," and they mentioned another name. Then one of them told me the whole history of the fuchsia—where it came from, how it had been developed, the different family names, and finally how we got this kind of particular fuchsia bush. But still we were no nearer to doing anything with the fuchsia.

So Margaret, who looked after the house, said, "Why don't you go up and ask Dan Archer." So I went up and got Dan Archer, and he trundled down and took one look at the fuchsia, its leaves and the bark, and then he said, "You know what? That needs a dose of Epsom salts." I suppose most of you know Epsom salts is for the stomach. And so, of course, we laughed long and loud, and then I said, "Now come off it, what does it really need?" "I am not joking, it needs a dose of Epsom salts. You give it one tablespoon of Epsom salts per day for four or five days and water it." "Well," I said, "I am not going to tell the whole company this; they will think I am crazy!" So I said to Margaret, "Margaret, it needs Epsom salts." And she said, "Don't be silly." I said, "Please, Dan Archer said it needs Epsom salts." So out she went and got the Epsom salts, and she said, "You can do it, not me." So I took the Epsom salts and watered it for three or four days and within two weeks that bush was back to normal and full of flowers. Do you see? The first two had knowledge but the third had wisdom. The first two knew all about the bush, they knew all the possibility of diseases, what this disease was, what that disease was, where it came from, its family background, all knowledge about it—fact after fact after fact. But old Mr. Dan Archer had wisdom; He knew what to do with the fact. He said, "That bush is diseased and I will tell you what to do. Use Epsom salts!" That was wisdom. And within a short time the thing was done.

You see, many Christians have knowledge. They know the facts, but they do not have wisdom. They do not know how to apply the facts. Some people know all about the church. They can tell you the foundation, the ground, the nature of the church, about being built together, the ministries of the church, the gifts of the church and everything else, but they do not have wisdom. They do not know how to apply the facts; how in fact, the facts can become experience. That is wisdom. Therefore get wisdom. May the Lord help us.

3.
Now is the Building of the House

II Chronicles 3:1–7

Then Solomon began to build the house of the Lord at Jerusalem on mount Moriah, where the Lord appeared unto David his father, which he made ready in the place that David had appointed, in the threshing-floor of Ornan the Jebusite. And he began to build in the second day of the second month, in the fourth year of his reign. Now these are the foundations which Solomon laid for the building of the house of God. The length by cubits after the first measure was threescore cubits, and the breadth twenty cubits. And the porch that was before the house, the length of it according to the breadth of the house, was twenty cubits, and the height a hundred and twenty; and he overlaid it within with pure gold. And the greater house he ceiled with fir-wood, which he overlaid with fine gold, and wrought thereon palm-trees and chains. And he garnished the house with precious stones for beauty: and the gold was gold of Parvaim. He overlaid also the house, the beams, the thresholds, and the walls thereof, and the doors thereof, with gold; and graved cherubim on the walls.

We have been looking at the two books of Chronicles and you will remember that Chronicles is one of those more unique books in the Bible, in that it is the interpretation of many other books. Just like Deuteronomy is the interpretation of the first four books of the Bible, so Chronicles is the interpretation of the whole of Old Testament history. This history is already recorded from Genesis right the way through to the end of Kings and indeed it goes beyond the end of Kings, it goes virtually to the coming of the Messiah. Within the book of Chronicles lies the secret behind all of God's dealings with men, and that is to have a habitation for Himself in the Spirit. His purpose is that He should not only save us, not only bring us into an experience of the indwelling Christ, not only bring us into an experience of the power of the Holy Spirit, but that we should be built together into a home of God in the Spirit, that we might grow into a holy temple in the Lord.

The Expression of the Building Work on Earth

I would like to go on to other things, but I feel somehow strangely held back. I have this matter on my heart, and I just have to trust the Lord to help me to express it. Let me first say this. When we come to II Chronicles 3, it tells us that Solomon began to build the house of the Lord in Jerusalem. I think we should be very careful of this kind of teaching that says all the building work is totally in the unseen. Of course, it is a spiritual work, but there is a kind of teaching which somehow seems to believe that all this takes place somehow or other in an abstract, vague, ethereal way. It does not matter how we live down here. We can be as divided as we wish to be, we can collide with one another and be out of sorts with one another as much as we wish, but somehow or other, in some marvelous way by grace we are all being built together in the unseen. It is an extraordinary kind of teaching and I must say a very comfortable one.

Now God preserve us from ever coming to another level than the one God would have us upon however difficult. The fact of the matter is this: of course this building is a spiritual building, of course it is essentially in the unseen at present. It is something which God is doing by His Spirit, and it is a habitation for God in the Spirit. But you know as well as I do that when a person gets saved, we expect to see some concrete results. If a person continues to live in sin and is born again we would doubt that he has actually been born again. If a person is really born of God we expect to see certain fruit. As the Lord Jesus said, by their fruit you shall know them as some positive expression of their spiritual birth. Spiritual things always have concrete expressions, and if God is building us together for an eternal habitation of Himself in the Spirit, then there will be some expression of that on earth. It will be spiritual; it will be of God; it will be of heaven; it will be by the Holy Spirit and through the ministry of the Holy

Spirit. You do not see the Holy Spirit, but it will nevertheless have concrete expression, and that is the first thing I would just like to underline.

Growing into a Holy Temple in the Lord

In Ephesians 2 it says, "Being built upon the foundation of the apostles and prophets, Christ Jesus himself being the chief corner stone;" *being built* "in whom each several building, fitly framed together, *groweth into a holy temple in the Lord;*" groweth into a holy temple in the Lord "in whom ye also are builded together for a habitation of God in the Spirit" (vv. 20–22).

In Ephesians 4 we read of gifts of men to the church. "And he gave some to be apostles; and some, prophets; and some, evangelists; and some, pastors and teachers; for the perfecting of the saints, unto the work of ministering, unto the building up of the body of Christ" (vv. 11–12). So this building up of the body of Christ is in time, on earth. It is in space; we are here in this dimension.

"But speaking truth in love, may grow up in all things into him, who is the head, even Christ; from whom all the body fitly framed and knit together through that which every joint supplieth, according to the working in due measure of each several part, maketh the increase of the body unto the building up of itself in love" (vv. 15–16).

1 Peter 2:4–5: "Unto whom coming, a living stone, rejected indeed of men, but with God elect, precious, ye also, as living stones, are built up a spiritual house, to be a holy priesthood,

to offer up spiritual sacrifices, acceptable to God through Jesus Christ." Ye also as living stones are built together. Ye also as living stones are built up a spiritual house.

When Brethren Come Together

And in 1 Corinthians 14:26: "What is it then, brethren? When ye come together, each one hath a psalm, hath a teaching, hath a revelation, hath a tongue, hath an interpretation. Let all things be done unto [building up]."

These scriptures show us that this building work has got to have a very concrete expression of it on earth. I cannot understand this kind of teaching that somehow or other we can drift through life as believers learning of the Lord, knowing the Lord in a totally personal way, and then suddenly in a twinkling of an eye when the Lord comes we are all built together as a habitation in a most marvelous and sudden dramatic way. The crabbiest and most awkward Christians suddenly get built together with others. I cannot understand it. We all know the kind of Christians who have spent their whole lives being awkward and difficult and self-centered, crabby is the best word for it, and we are to believe that suddenly in the twinkling of an eye they are marvelously changed and built together. Surely if there is going to be a building together, a work has got to take place here and now. It has to take place with us and the Holy Spirit has to do the work. This is not to say that it is not a personal work. It is a personal work; it is a deep work, and God uses one another to do the work.

The Inner Character of the King

There is a lot more we could say. In my heart I must say that if every Christian is going to sit on a throne and rule over this earth, God preserve us. That is the only thing I can say knowing some. If it really means that automatically just because we are saved every Christian is going to sit on a golden throne and rule areas of the earth, I must say the Lord preserve us. What kind of kingdom would that be? The Bible does not say that. It says, "If we suffer with Him we shall also reign with Him." There is an if. And the whole point is this: God never goes on title and position. He never goes on just something official. There is always character inside.

We see it most beautifully in our Lord Jesus Christ. Of course, He had the pedigree, of course, He was David's greater son, of course, the Bible takes great pains to point out that He is of the royal line of David, but the Father allowed the Lord Jesus to be divested of every single thing that this world calls royalty. He was divested of everything—all the mystique of royalty, all that sort of keeping at a distance, all that sort of outward dignity, all that goes with the aura of majesty. He was stripped naked, beaten black and blue, spat upon, the spittle covering His face, His beard was plucked out, a crown of thorns jammed on His head, a reed placed in His hand, almost unrecognizable as a human being, His visage more marred than any man. And in that moment the Lord Jesus was more King than at any other time in His whole life. His inner royalty came out. He made that crown of thorns the most precious crown that any man has ever worn. He made that reed the most powerful scepter that any king has ever held. Why? Because He had an inner quality that made Him worthy to be King. He is not simply King because He is of the Davidic line. He is King because He has the inner character of King and it has been proven that He is King—King of kings and Lord of lords.

If God would bring you and me to the throne by His grace alone, through the finished work of our Lord Jesus and by the ministry of the Holy Spirit, we too must have such an inner character of King in us. We will never be there just because we are called kings unto God. We must have the inner quality of the King. We must have the character of the King in us and this is true of everything else. It is true of the building work. If God is building living stones together on the foundation which is Jesus Christ, seeking to cause us to be fitly framed and knit together and to increase with the increase of God, this is not going to happen in the twinkling of an eye at the coming of the Lord. It has to happen now. The Holy Spirit has got to do something in us. We have to come to terms with one another however ugly and difficult "one another" may be. The fact of the matter is that we are stuck with each other and by the grace of God we have to go through with each other, and not just split and split and split again.

It is amazing to me to believe that one day we are all going to be this whole building fitly framed together growing into a holy temple in the Lord when we cannot bear each other down here. Only God can do a work in such a way in our hearts by His Spirit. First of all, our eyes need to be opened to see that this matter of being built together is not a luxury; it is an essential. If you and I are really going to be in this city, which is built together compact, if we are going to be the body of our Lord which is to grow up into

Him as Head in all things, if we are to be the bride of the Lord produced out of His life and character, if we are to be this holy temple of the Lord, then the work has got to be done down here in time and in space.

Mount Moriah

In II Chronicles 3 we find that Solomon began to build the house of the Lord in Jerusalem on Mount Moriah. And the scriptures made very much of this. You will remember that David found this spot as the site for the house of God through a sin which he had committed, and when finally he confessed, it was revealed to him that this was none other than the site of the house of God. And this is emphasized here in chapter 3 in this first verse that Mount Moriah was the place where the house of God was to be built.

Jehovah-jireh

What do we know about Mount Moriah? In Genesis 22 we read the very well-known story of Abraham offering up Isaac his son, which is a most wonderful picture of Calvary on which the Father offered up His only Son. You will note in Genesis 22:14 that an interpretation was given for Moriah. I do not understand the interpretation because Moriah in Hebrew does not mean quite what it says. The Bible says, "And Abraham called the name of that place Jehovah-jireh: as it is said to this day, in the mount of Jehovah it shall be provided." Moriah, according to many, means the "Lord provides." In the mount of the Lord it shall be provided. Isn't this marvelous! The Lord will provide.

Where does the Lord provide? Is it in some subjective experience of yours? Never! He provides through Calvary. He provides through the finished work of the Lord Jesus Christ, through the Son having been offered up by the Father for our sins. In the mount of the Lord it shall be provided, and the house of God is built on the mount in which it shall be provided. What shall be provided? Everything will be provided—our salvation, our sanctification, our anointing, all the materials for the building, the grace to sum up the work, to develop the work and to finish the work. In the mount of the Lord it shall be provided—Jehovah Jireh, the Lord will provide.

Do you realize that in the finished work of the Lord Jesus Christ, God has in one offering forever provided every single thing that any one of us needs to be saved, to serve God and to be built together in the Lord? Now some of you immediately say to me: "Just wait. What about Pentecost? Surely Pentecost is as important as Calvary." Of course Pentecost is as important as Calvary, it comes out of Calvary; it is the outflow of Calvary. I will come to that in a moment.

But a Thorn Bush

The first thing is that in the finished work of the Lord Jesus Christ every single thing that is required for the purpose of God to be fulfilled has been provided. I am a worthless bit of clay and so are you, dried up thorn bushes. Moses was a thorn bush; he was not a palm tree. What a wonderful thing it would have been if He had blazed forth in glory from the top of a stately palm tree in the

Sinai and said, "Moses, Moses, take off your shoes from off your feet. The ground where on thou standest is holy ground." The Lord would have looked down upon it. Absolutely magnificent!

I have often said that we Bible students would have a whale of a time taking the symbolism of a palm tree because it is engraved everywhere in the temple. Nor did the Lord take the acacia or the shittim tree which is the most common tree of all in the Sinai. This would have been a marvelous thing for Biblical expositors. "Why!" people would have said, "the tabernacle was made out of this, and in this the Lord appeared to Moses!" You see, He was telling him: "Moses, I am going to dwell in the midst of you." But God used the commonest bush of all, which was the thorn bush. Even the camels turn up their nose at the thorn bush. Furthermore, it was a dried up old thorn bush. It had lived its life and died. Its energy was burnt up; it was finished; it was dead. And into that dried up old thorn bush God Himself came and Moses later said, "The grace of Him that dwelt in the thorn bush." Out of that common, little, cheap, vulgar, ugly bush God chose to make one of the greatest encounters with any human being in world history. He said, "Moses, Moses, take the shoes from off thy feet for the ground whereon thou stands is holy ground." Holy ground!—a thorn bush?!

You and I are only thorn bushes. We think sometimes we are palm trees or acacia trees. We think we are something rather beautiful, something rather fine. But God says, "No, you are just a common thorn bush, two a pence; no good for anything; billions and billions of you. But the wonder is that God would say to Moses: "Moses, you are only a thorn bush. You thought you were a palm tree when you started out and slew that Egyptian and said you were to become a deliverer to the people of Israel. You thought you were a palm tree, but I reduced you to a thorn bush. It took Me forty years in the desert to reduce you to a thorn bush. Now Moses, I am going to get into you." The bush burned with fire and the bush was not consumed. You will remain what you are and I shall remain what I am; we together will do this work."

You and I are nothing, and sometimes it takes us a lifetime to discover that we are nothing, that we are only thorn bushes. We are not even olive trees until we are the thorn bush first. So if you want to be filled with the Spirit, first you have to become a thorn bush; then later you may become an olive tree. When you and I realize how utterly worthless we are, how insignificant we are, then this becomes real to us. How can I have any part in this building? How can I be built together as a habitation of God in the Spirit? I am only a common thorn bush. I am a worthless bit of clay, an insignificant bit of debris, but God says, "In the mount of the Lord it shall be provided through the finished work of the Lord Jesus Christ." He has clothed us with the garment of salvation and on top of that is the garment of praise. Then He says, "Now come into My presence with boldness, not because you are anything; you are still only an insignificant bit of clay, but now you are clothed in Jesus Christ." You can come into the presence of God clothed in the righteousness of the Lord Jesus Christ, dressed in all the excellencies of our God. He invites you to come before Him. He says, "Don't come in a shameful way, and don't come in apologizing. Come in with boldness, enter into My presence because in the mount of the Lord it shall be provided." Many believers think that justification belongs to the kindergarten. It does not! I believe that two-thirds of the problems among believers go back to the matter of justification, not sanctification, because so few people see what the Lord Jesus has done for them. Justification is a tremendous matter, and I have seen many saints delivered through simply seeing what the Lord Jesus has done for them. Justification is a tremendous matter, and I have seen many saints delivered through simply seeing what the Lord Jesus had done with their sin on the cross and what He had done with them through His crucifixion. In the mount of the Lord it shall be provided.

All the Building Materials are in Christ

You may be the most hopeless human being on this globe. You may be a person with a depraved background; you may be a person who is so unstable, but in the mount of the Lord it shall be provided. And if you will believe it and take the provision you shall come into the presence of the Lord and will be involved in the building work of God. And there is more than that; there is this whole matter of the indwelling of Christ. How can the Lord get into me and dwell in me? How can I know His resurrection life and power in me? In the mount of the Lord it shall be provided.

What is the problem? All the materials (we are talking spiritually) for the building of the house—gold, precious stones, silver, whatever it is—everything is Christ and all the qualities of Christ are in His eternal life and nature. The problem is to get His life flowing, and that is more than just being saved. Jesus said, "I am come that you might have life and that you might have it abundantly" (John 10:10). Once the life is flowing there will be the materials for the city. God begins to do the work in us of producing the materials for the city. But most of us feel: how could the Lord dwell in me? The problem is "I." The thing that dams up the whole life of God in us is our self-centeredness. We can get saved, but we can still be very self-centered. The whole world revolves around us. Everything revolves around me; I am the center. The Lord, heaven, the kingdom and the throne are all there for me.

Personal Testimony

When I was a young believer first saved, for four years I wrestled with this problem of "me." I tried to Christianize myself. I beat myself into prayer; I beat myself into Bible study; I beat myself into witnessing. The students at the college I attended were terrified of me. I would go to the student commons room and whenever I went down the corridor, everyone just vanished through the door. This was because I had adopted John Wesley's plan of talking to at least one person a day about their soul's salvation. I did it with great gusto, and the result was everyone was very afraid of me.

My problem was "self"; I could not get rid of myself. I tried to Christianize myself; I tried to make myself a really good Christian. I taught myself Biblical knowledge, I prayed, I witnessed and did everything until I felt hopeless. I will never forget the day when I saw two things. The first was this: the Spirit of God is in me to reproduce the character and life of the Lord Jesus. It was a revelation of God. What a fool I had been! If the Holy Spirit is in me, then why am I trying to do the work? If He is in me to reproduce the life of Christ, I have the key. I had locked Him up in the attic. I had been doing all the work without His help. Now He will do the work and I will cooperate.

The second thing was this, and it solved the whole problem for me: I saw that I was crucified with Christ. When Christ was crucified, I was crucified. It was not a matter of trying to be crucified nor was it a question of attaining unto it; I saw that it was done. The moment the Lord Jesus was crucified; Lance Lambert was crucified with Him; he died with Him. That was a revelation to me, and it was like a great load falling off my back. For the first time I became myself.

Believers Suffer from being Artificial

Most believers suffer from being artificial. It is not deliberate, but they have to try to be like the rest and it is awfully hard. You have to have that smile at the right time, you have to have that holy look at the right time, you have to say "amen" at the right time, you have to have the right Biblical words and the right phraseology or someone may pounce upon you to give you a lecture. It is a kind of artificiality. It is not that we deliberately want to be a hypocrite; we see we have been crucified with Christ and it is what Christ is in us that matters, then we can relax and become ourselves, warts and all. It is just as simple as that. We have come down to the level of reality. That does not mean you can inflict yourself on everybody. God will have to deal with you and me, but the fact is we are free to be ourselves. "I am what I am by the grace of God." And the apostle said in Romans 12:3: "For I say, through the grace that was given me, to every man that is among you, not to think of himself more highly than he ought to think; but so to think as to think soberly, according as God hath dealt to each man a measure of faith."

If your measure of faith is small, thank God for that. You have a measure of faith, let that be the real thing, for it is the only thing that matters. Don't try to inflate it. Don't try to create an artificial standard. Now in the mount of the Lord it shall be provided. If you have trouble with yourself, that is the problem.

The Problem in Being Built Together is the Big "I"

How can we all be built together when someone says, "I", and someone else says "I," and someone else says, "I." "I" is the problem. I feel; I know; I disagree; I have it from the Lord. "I" is all over the place. How can you bind the "I"s together? But when you say, "I have been crucified with Christ, nevertheless I live, yet not I but Christ," and another "I" can say, "Not I but Christ," and another says, "Not I but Christ," then there is a blending. It is not that we lose our originality or our personality. These things are given to us by God to be broken and then to be molded and to come into their own. There is a right spontaneity. And may God get us all there for the right kind of living and normal life. But the fact that it is Christ—Christ in you; Christ is the power and the dynamic. In the mount of the Lord it shall be provided

Bear in Our Body the Dying of Jesus

Do you have a problem with yourself? Thank God He has crucified you with Christ. In the mount of the Lord it shall be provided. The moment you go down, the life of God starts to flow.

"He that believeth on me, from within him shall flow out rivers of living water" (see John 7:38). All you have to do is believe into Him, believe on Him, and rivers of living water will flow out. You die and out comes the life. "Always bearing about in the body the dying of Jesus, that the life also of Jesus may be manifested in our body" (II Corinthians 4:10). We have this treasure in earthen vessels. We have the treasure inside if Christ is within, but how can the treasure within come out? How can it be contributed? Only when we bear in our body the dying of Jesus can the life also be manifested. So then death works in us, but life in you is contributed—death in us, life in you. If every one of us knew an experience of that, wouldn't it be marvelous? Every one of us would be building one another up.

I think you have heard the old Jewish story of the rabbi who had a dream and saw in the kingdom of heaven a whole number of people sitting around a table eating. An angel brought the food and put it in each of their bowls and then brought them spoons to eat with that were two yards long. They had a terrible time trying to eat. As he took up his spoon to eat the handle would run into the eye of the one next to him. Suddenly one of them started to feed the man opposite, and then they all began to feed one another, and there was no longer a problem. That is the kingdom of heaven. There is a lesson here for you and me. It means simply that if we would all know what it is to be crucified with Christ, then in the mount of the Lord it shall be provided. If we are denied any experience then it will be death in us and life in you, and every one of us would be giving life to the rest. Think what that would be.

The Anointing of the Holy Spirit

What about the anointing of the Holy Spirit? There is an anointing of the Holy Spirit, and make no mistake about that. There is a real anointing of the Holy Spirit. There is a power and empowering of the Holy Spirit that comes upon us. This also is through the finished work of the Lord Jesus Christ. Acts 2:32–33 says: "This Jesus did God raise up, whereof we all are witnesses. Being therefore by the right hand of God exalted, and having received of the Father the promise of the Holy Spirit, he hath poured forth this, which ye see and hear."

Who has received the promise of the Father? The Lord Jesus, not you or me, but the Lord Jesus has received the promise of the Father. What is the promise of the Father? The promise of the Father is the promise of the Holy Spirit. How has the Lord Jesus received the promise of the Father? Through His finished work He has appeared before the face of God for us. The Lord Jesus did not need the promise of the Holy Spirit. He was already born of the Spirit and anointed with the Spirit, and by the Spirit He offered Himself up to God without spot or blemish on the cross. Through the Spirit He was raised from the dead. It says, "The Spirit of Him that raised up Christ Jesus dwells in you." So He did not need the promise of the Father. For whom then did He receive this promise? For you and me, and He received it on the basis of His finished work. So you can strive and strive and strain and strain, but you will never enter into the empowering of the Holy Spirit until you see that it is your birthright and it belongs to you through the finished work of the Lord Jesus. In the mount of the Lord it shall be provided!

We need the Holy Spirit if we are going to know what it is to be built together, if we are going to know both the clothing and the equipment for the building work. We need to know every single aspect of the work of God.

Ornan's Threshing Floor

Will you also note that this house is built on Ornan's threshing floor (see II Chronicles 3). I wonder why it makes so much of Ornan's threshing floor. There is one thing that comes to me in a very solemn way and it is this: If there is to be any building there can be no sin. Ornan's threshing floor was the scene of one of David's collapses. He numbered the people of God and it was there he saw the angel of the Lord standing with his sword unsheathed ready to wreak havoc in Jerusalem. And the prophet Gad went to David and said, "David, you have sinned. The Lord has offered three things from which you may choose one that can be done to you." You might remember that I have already said: answers reveal the kind of person you are even in your sins. When Gad said this to David, he said, "I will not choose, let the Lord choose. It is better to fall into the hands of the living God." And the Lord chose.

Now this teaches us from I Chronicles 21 a very real but simple lesson. The altar was built on the site of the threshing floor which means there is a threshing floor connected with building. God has to thresh us, and I say this to myself. Where there is sin, it has to be confessed, and once it is confessed there is the threshing. What does God do in threshing? He separates the chaff from the wheat. A good example of this is in Luke 22:31: "Simon, Simon, behold, Satan asked to have you, that he might sift you as wheat: but I made supplication for thee, that thy faith fail not; and do thou, when once thou hast turned again, establish thy brethren."

Satan asks to have you that he might sift you as wheat. That is exactly what we find in 1 Chronicles 21. Satan got permission to do something and he caused David to number the people of God. The greatest among us can fall, but then there has to be this threshing. A wonderful thing of course is that in the end Satan gets the chaff and God gets the wheat. C.T. Studd once said, "Satan is God's greatest servant because God uses him more than anyone else to do His work."

Once sin is confessed then the scene becomes the place of building. If there is sin in your life, get it settled. Otherwise, it will effectively put you out of the building. Get it settled, and when it is settled, then the very scene of your sin will become the scene of the building. The grace of God is so great, so infinite that He turns the whole thing round and makes the scene of your fall the scene of your being built into God's home in the Spirit. May the Lord help us.

The Building and Living Sacrifices

When David saw this in Ornan's threshing floor, he offered up burnt offerings. He would not offer them free; he paid for them. This comes to a simple little matter: You can know all about this matter of the church, you can know about being built together, you can know all about fellowship and other things pertaining to building, but unless you are prepared to be a burnt offering, unless you are prepared to present your body a living sacrifice unto God, holy and acceptable to Him, there will be no building. There can be no building. The church was never a platform for our ministries. The church was never just a place for the exhibition of our gifts. The church was never a place for self-satisfaction and self-fulfillment. The church is to be a home for God in the Spirit, and the gateway into it is that we must lay down our lives. That is why I find I John 3:16 very remarkable. We all know John 3:16, but I John 3:16 seems to be the marvelous complement to it: "Hereby know we love, because he laid down his life for us: and we ought to lay down our lives for the brethren." Only when we are prepared to lay down our lives can there be a building. Have you laid down your life?

The House is Built on the Foundation

The last point I would like to make is that this house is built on the foundation. That seems to be quite a simple statement. In II Chronicles 3:3a it says, "Now these are the foundations which Solomon laid for the building of the house of God." The rabbis tell us that a large portion of Mount Moriah was leveled in order to lay this foundation. It was a very big job. A huge platform of stone was laid upon Mount Moriah. Only one crag was left exactly as it was and that is literally where Ornan's threshing floor was. The rest was leveled and huge stones, enormous blocks were laid into position making it a very great and solid foundation. And God has laid for us a very great and solid foundation. In I Corinthians 3:11 we read: "For other foundation can no man lay than that which is laid, which is Jesus Christ." Here is our foundation, a sure and certain foundation. It has been laid by God and no one can undo it. And the building has got to take place on that foundation.

The Foundation of the Church

The basis of all God's building work is on that foundation which is Jesus Christ. The basis of all our fellowship is Jesus Christ. What is the foundation upon which you are meeting together wherever you meet? Whether it is in homes, in halls, large meetings or small meetings, what is the foundation? Is it something less than God's foundation? Or is it something more than God's foundation? If it is less than God's foundation, God will not build. If it is more than God's foundation, God will not build. It must be exactly on the foundation of God. What is the foundation of God? Jesus Christ and Him crucified. That is the foundation of God.

Jesus Christ and Him Crucified

The apostle Paul says in 1 Corinthians 2: "I determined not to know anything among you, save Jesus Christ and him crucified" (v. 2). He says, "That is my basis. I am not going to discuss Peter's party or Apollos' party or the exclusive party or my own party which I am afraid has been formed around me. I am here to know Jesus Christ and Him crucified. And for you who say you belong to Peter's party, I ignore that. They are my brothers and sisters. I refuse to say you belong to St. Peter! And I refuse to accept that they belong to Apollos' teaching ministry—his conference center. No, no! You are mine and I am yours because you are in

Christ and that is the foundation of God. And even those who say, "We are the church, the exclusives, I am of Christ." And they put a little rope around themselves and say, "The rest of you are outside because you are a bit unclean. When we have inspected you, we will get you in, if we feel you have passed the test." "Oh!" says the apostle Paul, "that is narrower than God." All these others are still in Christ. God has not ejected them. They have added more to the foundation, Jesus Christ plus Apollos' emphasis, Jesus Christ plus Paul's revelations. None of it is the church! The foundation is Jesus Christ, and that is the basis.

Our basis must not be teaching, methods, technique, personalities, tradition, experiences as such. The teachings may even be very Biblical. I have known companies to divide on small details about whether we are going to go through the tribulation or not. If the Lord had wanted to clear up this problem, He could have given us a very clear chapter on whether we would go through the tribulation or not. But He did not! Why? Because He wanted to confuse us. He wanted to keep us in a state of confusion over this matter so that we are on our tiptoes. The Lord might come any time and the whole emphasis of the Word of God is: "Watch and pray." We are not to be absorbed in whether we are going to go through or whether we are going before or whether we are going during or whether it is going to be a half rapture or complete rapture. Of course, we have our own theories about these matters, but they are not causes for division.

If someone speaks in tongues, praise God. Hallelujah! Let them speak in tongues provided it is the real thing; it is of God. We are not to divide on someone who speaks in tongues. People sometimes come and say, "They speak with tongues in

Richmond." That evidently is the most terrible thing in the whole world. So when they ask I always refuse to answer. So what! Actually we do not have such a lot of it publicly. But we would not forbid it: we just go on. And there are many other things too. You cannot just cut a line and say, "You speak in tongues! Out! You have been baptized—again? Out!" You cannot do it. Has God received them? You see the basis? The extent?

Receive One Another as Christ Also Received You

The basis for fellowship is Romans 15:7: "Wherefore receive ye one another, even *as Christ also received you,* to the glory of God." [Speaker's emphasis] How did God receive you? He received you as a sinner saved by His grace. That was the minimum; that is how He saved you. That is how He saved me. He did not save me as a going-on saint. He did not say, "Ah, now if you are going to go right on, I will save you. You really are going to receive burial baptism? Right, I will save you. You will go right on to this? All right I will save you." No, I just made a little weak cry and prayed the most unscriptural prayer that is possible. I said, "Oh God, if there is a God, will you please do in me what you did in (somebody else I mentioned)." It was a very unscriptural prayer. But God saved me. Now if God received me on that basis, what about you? Will you receive me on that basis? Or will you say, "No, no, he should not have said that. He should have prayed the scripture that says, 'You cannot come to God unless you believe He is.'" So we do not accept him, he is suspect. He is definitely suspect. God received me. If God received me, can you not receive me? You say, "No, no, we have to be careful." Very well then, I am in a most extraordinary position. The God of all heaven has received me, and you who have been saved by the same work that saved me, will not receive me. What can we do?

Don't Investigate One Another's Conscience

It also says in Romans 14:1: "But him that is weak in faith receive ye, yet not for decision of scruples." The more modern version puts it like this: "investigation of his conscience." Oh, wonderful word! Don't we investigate one another's conscience? "Does he smoke? Oh, I will give him a little track about lung cancer on smoking." "Is he worldly? Oh, my word! Well, we will invite him to supper and get so and so to give his testimony. Or we will arrange things beautifully so it will be spontaneous." And the poor person is nearly dying a million deaths while we investigate his conscience. God has not raised this problem, but we do. Before the Holy Spirit even so much as breathed about this, we are blowing like a gale on them. "Now look here: have you come into this experience? Have you come into that experience? It will change your life. You have got to have it!" Why don't we let God do His work? Why don't we love one another? Why don't we receive one another? Why don't we care for one another? The most helpful people whom I have ever known have been the people who have received me just as I am in the Lord. And then you do not feel that you are being manipulated or pushed and pressurized. You are just yourself and you can grow in the Lord. And when a problem comes, you can go to those people and ask them. Or when they do speak to you, you are thankful for it. How lovely real fellowship is.

The apostle Paul put it again in Philippians 3:15: "Let us therefore, as many as are perfect, be thus minded: and if in anything ye are otherwise minded, this also shall God reveal unto you." Don't argue about it. He talked about something that would have put him quite honestly, if it was not in Scripture, out of many fellowships. How can he talk about winning Christ when you are already saved? How can he talk about out-resurrection from the dead? That sounds dangerous. And attaining to it? Don't we all get raised willy-nilly? What is he talking about? No wonder all the churches in Asia turned away from him. But he says, "I am not going to argue about this matter. Those of us who are going right on with the Lord are thus minded. But if any of you are otherwise minded, this also will God reveal. Leave it to God. 'Only, whereunto we have attained, by that same rule let us walk'" (v. 16) If God has dealt with you about certain things, never go back on it. Walk according to the rule whereunto God has brought you. And for someone who has just come in, don't try to sort of propel them unto your rule. Do not do it; let them grow. Sometimes with those of us who are older, the best way for the cross to work in us is to take our hands off another's life. There is so much flesh in those of us who are older in the Lord, and we do not even realize it. Our clammy hands get on a poor young believer and we try to manipulate him, push him or engineer him.

Now someone will say, "Aren't we to care for one another?" Of course we are to care for one another. We are to love one another. I want to suggest that if we really loved one another we would not try to manipulate them. If we really prayed for one another as much as the Lord prays for us, I think we would have a tender sensitiveness for one another. We would receive one another as the Lord has received us.

In Christ—Our Foundation for Gathering Together

What is this foundation? Christ. I am in Christ; he is in Christ; he is in Christ; he is in Christ. Do we all have tailor-made Christs? No. Do I have a Lutheran Christ? A Methodist Christ? An Episcopalian Christ? A Baptist Christ? A Brethren Christ? So now we have these differences. No, we have not. There is only one Christ. He is neither Catholic, Protestant, Lutheran, Episcopalian, Brethren nor exclusive. He is the Christ and we are all in that Christ.

Then he says, "Ah, but Christ lives in me." And another one says, "That is extraordinary; He lives in me!" Another one says, "Well, I have made a new discovery; He lives in me also." So what is happening? We are all in the one Christ and the one Christ is in all of us. Here is our foundation. This is the foundation for our gathering together. Whatever it is—small meetings, large meetings, home meetings, meetings in halls, whatever it is, our foundation is the Lord Jesus Christ. And we are to find one another in Him and love everybody who is really born of Him. It is inclusive of everyone born of God and exclusive of everyone who is not. That is our foundation. May the Lord help us, and may we know what it is to find that in the mount of the Lord it is provided. It is all provided in and through the finished work of our Lord Jesus Christ.

4.
Materials for the House

II Chronicles 3:1–9

Then Solomon began to build the house of the Lord at Jerusalem on mount Moriah, where the Lord appeared unto David his father, which he made ready in the place that David had appointed, in the threshing-floor of Ornan the Jebusite. And he began to build in the second day of the second month, in the fourth year of his reign. Now these are the foundations which Solomon laid for the building of the house of God. The length by cubits after the first measure was threescore cubits, and the breadth twenty cubits. And the porch that was before the house, the length of it, according to the breadth of the house, was twenty cubits, and the height a hundred and twenty; and he overlaid it within with pure gold. And the greater house he ceiled with fir-wood, which he overlaid with fine gold, and wrought thereon palm-trees and chains. And he garnished the house with precious stones for beauty: and the gold was gold of Parvaim. He overlaid also the house, the beams, the thresholds, and the walls thereof, and the doors thereof, with gold; and graved cherubim on the walls.

And he made the most holy house: the length thereof, according to the breadth of the house, was twenty cubits, and the breadth thereof twenty cubits; and he overlaid it with fine gold, amounting to six hundred talents. And the weight of the nails was fifty shekels of gold. And he overlaid the upper chambers with gold.

II Chronicles 5:6–9, 13–14

And king Solomon and all the congregation of Israel, that were assembled unto him, were before the ark, sacrificing sheep and oxen, that could not be counted nor numbered for multitude. And the priest brought in the ark of the covenant of the Lord unto its place into the oracle of the house, to the most holy place, even under the wings of the cherubim. For the cherubim spread forth their wings over the place of the ark, and the cherubim covered the ark and the staves thereof above. And they drew out the staves so that the ends of the staves were seen from the ark before the oracle; but they were not seen without: and there it is unto this day.

It came to pass, when the trumpeters and singers were as one, to make one sound to be heard in praising and thanking the Lord; and when they lifted up their voice with the trumpets and cymbals and instruments of music, and praised the Lord, saying, For he is good; for his lovingkindness endureth for ever; that then the house was filled with a cloud, even the house of the Lord, so that the priests could not stand to minister by reason of the cloud: for the glory of the Lord filled the house of God.

The two books of Chronicles are one of the most vital parts of the Word of God. There are some books which interpret all the other books. Deuteronomy is one and interprets the first four books of the Bible. And Chronicles interpret the whole of the Old Testament going right back to Adam, covering all the ground that has already been covered in the other books, especially the two books of Samuel, the two books of Kings and going right on to the return from Babylon virtually to the coming of the Messiah. These two books of Chronicles, along with Ezra and Nehemiah which are an old Jewish order, were linked together. These books covered all that and they were interpretations of all that God had been doing. In other words, we are introduced here in these two books and Ezra and Nehemiah to the very secret of God's heart. We are introduced to the yearning of His heart, to that thing for which He has longed for His own from eternity to eternity. And what is it?

Living Stones for the Habitation of God in the Spirit

We read, of course, in Ephesians 2 that we being fitly framed together might grow into a holy temple in the Lord—not only a temple of the Lord but a holy temple in the Lord (see v. 21). So glorious is this! "In whom we are also to be builded together for a habitation of God in the Spirit" (v. 22). In other words, the secret of human history—the secret of redemption, all that lies behind God's dealings with man, His so great salvation, His gift of the Holy Spirit—all His ways are that He might have a home for Himself in the Spirit. And the wonder of wonders is that you and I are that home. We are the living stones. We are the material that God has so gloriously saved. Isn't it wonderful when you see the whole Bible from beginning to end? In the first three chapters and the last three chapters we find they correspond, and then we realize the amazing and marvelous grace of God. He could have finished with us all. He could have finished with Adam and Eve when they fell and said, "Right out! Finished! We will just dynamite them and start again, and we will have a new Adam and Eve." No, God is not like that. God has worked unceasingly to retrieve what He has lost, to recover what He has lost, to bring back what He has lost, to reconcile what He has lost. And you and I are the fruit of that reconciliation, that work of the Lord Jesus Christ in bringing us back to God. But what a tragedy it is when we make our so great salvation the end, when it is but a means to the end of coming back into God's original purpose for mankind. And His original purpose was that we might be joined to Him, becoming partakers of the divine nature in order that we may be joined together into a holy temple in the Lord—a place where God manifests Himself, where He expresses Himself, where He comes home, where His glory is revealed.

The Lord Will Provide

Then we spoke about Moriah and Jehovah-jireh, "the Lord will provide," the place where Abraham offered his only son up to God, the son who was born of promise; Moriah, in the mount of the Lord it shall be provided. We saw that God has provided every single thing that sinners need to be saved through the work of the Lord Jesus Christ. And more than that; every single thing that sinners, who are saved, need to serve God has been provided through the finished work of the Lord Jesus Christ. Every single thing that He has required for the building of the house of God or the construction, as it were, of this holy temple in the Lord has been provided. The indwelling of the Holy Spirit, the empowering of the Holy Spirit, the anointing of the Holy Spirit, the gifts of the Holy Spirit have all been provided on the basis of the finished work of the Lord Jesus Christ. You may be the most insignificant person in the whole world, you may be the most worthless believer in the whole world, but if you are a believer you have a glorious birthright. Everything is given to you by grace through faith if you will only enter in. God has done it for you and given it to you through the finished work of His dear Son.

The Foundation

Then we spoke about the foundation. What a huge foundation it was. The whole of the top of Mount Moriah was leveled except for that one crag which still sticks out on that side to this very day and was the place of the threshing floor of Ornan the Jebusite. Huge stones were laid in place for that foundation. And we know that the foundation is Jesus Christ and Him crucified. There is no other foundation, and the devil works unceasingly to have a foundation for our coming together and for our being built together apart from that foundation. We like to mix unbelievers with believers, but we cannot do it. We like to make it less than the Lord Jesus Christ, but we cannot do it. The foundation is Jesus Christ and Him crucified.

Then the most common thing is to add to the foundation—the foundation plus baptism, the foundation plus an experience of holiness, the foundation plus the baptism of the Spirit, the foundation plus the gifts of the Spirit, the foundation plus some interpretation of prophecy, the foundation plus an interpretation of something else. And we say, "If you would be with us, come in, come in. The rest of you are visitors. You can sit at the back and be spectators, but you are not in the inner circle." That is the foundation plus. But God's foundation is Jesus Christ and Him crucified, and on that foundation God builds. Now the Holy Spirit refuses to commit Himself when there is less than the foundation or more than the foundation. He is paralyzed. He will bless people as saints; He will use them as saints, but the building work of God is paralyzed. He will not build until He has the right foundation. He must have the right foundation. It is so important for us all to see this simple matter that whether we are meeting in homes, in halls, large companies or small companies, our foundation must be Jesus Christ. This finds us out because it means we have to receive everyone whom Christ has received. Oh dear, we do have some problems. Someone comes along and someone whispers, "Popery; away!" And then someone else comes along and someone whispers, "Oh, Baptists." Someone else comes along and we say, "Watch out, exclusives." And we have problems when we begin to receive all that Christ receives. Nevertheless, if Christ has received you, I must receive you. How can I be at loggerheads with my Lord? If He has received you, I must receive you. I may not like the look of your face, but I have to receive you. We have to be built together. It is not a question of color, race, nationality or social class; it is a question of whether Christ has received you. If He has received you, you are my brother. I cannot do anything about it. And I am your brother and you cannot do anything about it. You are my sister, and I am your brother. We cannot do anything about it. I have a sister, but I cannot change her. She is my sister; I cannot help it. She came along and I am numbered with her. We have brothers and sisters in the Lord and we have got to receive them as Christ has received us. That is the foundation.

The First Thing in the Building are the Stones

Now I want to share a little more about the materials that were used in this building, but I can only touch on it here. The amazing thing is that God went to all this trouble to get these stones built together and then He covered the whole lot up. Think of that! He went to all that trouble to quarry these stones without sound of hammer or chisel or any such thing, brought them to their place, numbered them, fitted them beautifully together, and then covered the whole lot up first with wood, then with gold and then with precious stones. And anyone who came in would not even know that there were stones in the building. When they looked up, gold; they looked down, gold; they looked that way, gold; they looked every way, gold. They saw no stones because they were all hidden. Only God could do that. We would have wanted to leave those stones uncovered, or we would say to the Lord,

"Now Lord, do not bother too much about these stones; they are all going to be covered up anyway. If there are chinks and cracks in them, do not bother too much about them because they are going to be covered by wood, then by gold, then by precious stones. That which everyone will see are the precious stones and the gold. They are going to see those lovely engravings of cherubim, lilies and palm trees. They are not going to bother with what is behind them, so don't go to too much trouble with the stones. Tell the workmen, 'Now boys, just get on and do the work, but do not get too worried about the stones because no one is going to see them.'" But not the Lord. The first thing about this building are the stones.

Stones from Deep Under the Ground

Let me tell you a few things about these stones. First they were quarried, and the scripture from 1 Kings 6 and 7 says that there was no sound, hammer or chisel, so generally we think they were all quarried miles away from the temple site. But in Mount Moriah there are huge caverns under it. I have been there many times and have seen the huge chisel marks deep down in the earth where enormous blocks of stone, sometimes thirty-two feet long, nine feet high and nine feet wide, have been chiseled out. It was deep under the ground and hidden. That is why no one could hear the hammer or the chisel. But it was out of Mount Moriah that probably much of the stone was taken and maybe from another quarry some little distance away that was also used. But very much of the large stones were quarried out of Mount Moriah, which means they were cut roughly. That is the first thing.

The Stones Were Polished, Beveled and Marked

Then the stones were dressed which means they were polished, and it was a big job. Then the edges were beveled. You can see on the very old stones still to this day the way that they were beveled around the edges. Then they were marked while they were still in the quarry. The rabbis, especially Josephus the late Jewish historian of the time of our Lord, said, "So beautiful were the stones that they marked them in such a way that the grain ran right through the stones. It was just like a flower or a plant in its beauty. The whole thing was forecast. Now I could take you today, not to the Solomonic stones but to other stones that came in a later period of time in Jerusalem, and I could show you stones much higher than myself and quite long and you cannot get a knife between them. All the years that have gone by with earthquakes and other storms have moved these stones closer together so that you cannot get a knife between them. There are certain places that have a warning to stay away and the doves have gotten in there and are building a nest.

Generally speaking, there was no water or cement, but these stones were so perfectly cut, so perfectly dressed and numbered that they fitted together so that you could actually see the grain running through them. All that work and God covers it up. God sees it, but it is not seen with the naked eye.

Born-again Believers Are Living Stones

You and I are living stones. And it says in I Peter 2:4–5: "Unto whom coming [the Lord Jesus], a living stone, rejected indeed of men, but with God elect, precious, ye also, as living stones, are built up a spiritual house, to be a holy priesthood, to offer up spiritual sacrifices, acceptable to God through Jesus Christ."

You and I are living stones. Did you know that? If you are a born-again believer let it get into your heart by the Spirit of God that you are a living stone. If you are born of God, if you are saved by the grace of God, you are a living stone. God has quarried you out of the nature of Christ. Out of His own life, He has quarried you. You have been taken out and are born of God. He has begotten you again to a living hope by the resurrection of Jesus Christ from the dead. You have something of His life in you. You have something of His nature in you. You have been quarried; you are a living stone, quarried out of the rock-like nature and life of God.

One Stone Never Makes a House

What is the point of a living stone? If I were to take you to my home and show you the foundation with one stone on it and say this is my home, surely you would think I was crazy. It might be a magnificent stone, a beautiful stone, cut, polished, dressed, beveled, and with beautiful grain, but one stone has never made a house. Even if it is a beautiful stone of great proportions, magnificent, beautifully prepared, but one stone never makes a house. Oh, there are so many believers just like that. They are solitary; they are all on their own. "I have everything," they say, "I have the Lord; blessed be His name." They are one solid piece of stone, cut, and dressed, but they are in solitary beauty. And God says, "What can I do with this stone?" It has everything; the stone believes, it can praise Him, go on with Him; it is self-sufficient. But what is the point of a living stone? There must be other stones.

Piles of Stone Do Not Make a House

On the other hand, if I took you to the foundation and there were a great number of stones all over the place, and I said, "Come in, this is my house," you would still think I was crazy. There may be two hundred stones, but that is not a house. They are all in a tumbled mess everywhere, and you say, "This is not a house." Oh, yes, it is; what else do you make the house of? (Of course, in the United States you make houses of wood so this does not mean so much here.)

Where we come from there are many houses of stone, but a great pile of stones does not make a house. Even if someone has tidied up the stones and put them all in piles one on top of the other, this way and that way, that is not a house even though they are on the foundation. There are believers who are just a mass of stones together, saying, "We are the church; we are the church. Of course, we are the church; what else is the church made of?" But we have to be built together to become the house of the Lord. We cannot be the home of God in the Spirit unless we are built together. Of course, sometimes people have gotten busy and tidied up the stones and have them all together in piles. There is some kind of fellowship and some kind of order, but it is still not the house of God because it is not according to the Holy Spirit's sovereignty. It is according to man's idea of doing it, and that is still not the house of the Lord.

What has to happen to those stones on the right foundation? They have to find their right relationship to one another, so stone after stone finds its proper place in its relationship to other stones. The whole house begins to grow and it does not matter where you are in the house. You are somewhere and you are there by God's appointment, and because you are there you have a responsibility for the whole. Now that is what it means to be built up a spiritual house. That is what it means to be fitly framed together.

Togetherness

Will you notice just three things about this "together"? In Ephesians 2:21b it says, "Fitly framed together." 22a: "In whom ye also are builded together." 4:16a: "From whom all the body fitly framed and knit together."

The stones have to be together, and it has to be the Spirit who fits them together. It does not come academically; it does not come mentally; it is only the Holy Spirit who can create this togetherness, this sense of belonging. It is a wonderful thing when you at last see: "I belong. I belong to the Lord, therefore I belong to these people." All the way through the scriptures you will find togetherness. Of course, every one of us has to have their own life with the Lord. This is where others have made a mistake. You will remember that the boards in the tabernacle each had two little sockets that each board stood on; it had its own two feet.

And then it had a pole that ran right through, joining it together with all the others. That is togetherness. You have your own two feet which means you have your own life with the Lord, your own walk with the Lord, and your own original experience from the Lord, but you must be together. The two feet must go hand in hand; your own life together with the others.

Relatedness

The second thing is relatedness. They find their relationship to one another in the Lord and it is God's choice. Every one of these stones are numbered. Now we do not always like this. We like to sort of find people that we feel are amenable to us, that are pleasant, we see eye to eye with, and then we say we are going to be one with them; I can be built with them. But God does not do it that way. God says, "No, the grain has got to go through the stone and you may well find the thing you do not like about brother so and so is the very thing that is in you; it is the grain. "Oh," you say, "I cannot bear that." But the Lord puts you together and you have to stay there. This is the way we learn Christ. We do not learn Christ in books; we do not learn Christ in lovely meetings where we are left untouched. We learn Christ through the discipline of being together and sooner or later the people in the church will say something about you that you will resent very deeply and then you will get up and walk out and say, "That's the end. Anyway I have been thinking for some time that this lot was not too spiritual. The Lord is leading me somewhere else where the fellowship is of a deeper kind." You cannot do that. They may be wrong, but there is an opportunity for you to die. If you have lost your reputation what a blessed thing it is. You have nothing more to defend. Most of us have a façade because of a certain reputation that we are trying to keep. We are projecting something and we want to keep this projection. So we spend all our life trying to keep up this façade. Of course, God cannot do much with a façade. He has to get to us behind the façade. Therefore, when someone says something about your reputation, what a wonderful thing that is! Thank them.

There was an older brother in Denmark, Christenson, who was a very, very brave man of God. He was once very upset about something that someone said about him, and he went to the Lord to complain about it, and the Lord said, "This person is your very great friend, for he is keeping you humble." So he said, "Lord, I will give a five krona piece (probably equivalent of a dollar today) to anyone who criticizes me." And he did that all through his life. When people came to him and said, "Brother, I thought you were a bit long today," he would solemnly take out his purse and say, "Here you are; you shall have this. Thank you for keeping me humble."

You should be very thankful for this because in many ways this is the way God deals with us. This is the way stones are built together and we get to know each other. In a family relationship, whether it is brothers and sisters, husband and wife, children and parents, don't we learn this? Some of you who are parents know this. Parents often say to me, "My children say, 'You are so old fashioned.'" And then parents resent it. You are probably getting old, so the kids keep you young. We do this all the time in relationships. We can either resent it, walk out or accept it. But this is the way we get to know ourselves. We must get to know ourselves. If we do not we shall never know the Lord. When we know the Lord, we get to know ourselves. And more often than not the way you get to know yourself is not by some glorious mountain-top experience where the Lord embraces you to Himself. It is somewhere down here in team work and someone says something about you that you do not like.

Jacob the Supplanter

I have often told you about Jacob whose name means "twister or deceiver." In Hebrew it is really twister because when he was born his arm was round his brother's leg, and they said he twisted his arm round his brother's leg. So they called him "supplanter, twister." He was the biggest swindler in the Middle East, but he did not know it. When he stole his brother's birthright, he did not realize it. When he stole his brother's blessing, he did not realize it. He was just doing what comes naturally. His thought was: "In the name of the Lord if my brother does not care for the blessing, why should I not have it? He never bothered too much about it, so I should have it." How did the Lord cure him? He sent him to the second biggest swindler in the Middle East, his Uncle Laban. He was right in the family. These two swindled each other for twenty-one years. I know it sounds awful, but if you take your rose colored spectacles off and read the Bible slowly, you will see how those two swindled each other for twenty-one years until Jacob became sick to death—not of his uncle but of himself.

First it was Leah, and she was in on that swindle. The father could not have dressed her up and said, "Now you just keep quiet; don't you give the game away. If you have to say anything at all just make a peep. Walk like your sister, act like your sister, do everything like your sister." It was only when Jacob lifted the veil that he found out it was not Rachel. Poor Jacob; swindled! Can you believe what he thought about his uncle? "How could a person swindle his own flesh and blood?" But Jacob had swindled his own flesh and blood, his twin brother. Later on, of course, Rachel did the same thing. He never thought that Rachel was capable of having an evil thought, but she was. When they left home for the last time, Uncle Laban came out in hot fury and stopped the whole caravan and said, "You have stolen the household gods." Jacob was thunderstruck. Household gods! Me? Never! Search everything! Of course, when they came to dear Rachel, she was sitting on the camel on the saddle, and she said, "I do not feel too well; don't, father, ask me to come down." And he did not; however, under the saddle were all the household gods.

Jacob Saw Himself

Jacob saw himself in three ways. He saw himself first in his Uncle Laban, then in Leah, then in Rachel. He got nearer and nearer to himself till finally he was so sick of himself that when the Lord met him at the ford Jabbok, he would not let Him go until He changed him from Jacob into Israel. That is what God does with living stones. Don't ever think you are going to get away from the dealings of the Lord in this matter. He puts you with someone and you discover the same thing in yourself. You may not be given to swindling, but it will be something else. Maybe you are proud; maybe you are very self-opinionated; perhaps you are long-winded. But you can be sure that the Lord will put you with someone and you will see it so clearly in the end. Suddenly you cry out to the Lord: "Lord, deliver me from this thing. I see it so beautifully in brother so and so." Oh, how we love each other when we come to see that we are all the same in the end, and God builds us until we find our relationship in one another in the Lord—fitly framed together. We are fitted together in such a way that we become an integral part of the building. And it does not matter where you are so long as you are somewhere between the foundation and the top stone. That is all that matters; you are in the building.

Being Built Together Means Discipline

Therefore there are one or two things about this matter. The first thing is the discipline. Are we ready for the discipline of being built together? I find sometimes that there is a certain kind of teaching that seems to preach a freedom from all discipline and responsibility. This is entirely anti-scriptural. To be free from bondage, to be free from division, to be free from self-consciousness; this is freedom. But the greatest freedom any man or woman can have is the freedom to be a prisoner in the Lord Jesus Christ. Remember that the apostle Paul says in Ephesians 3:1: "I the prisoner of the Lord Jesus Christ." Then he goes into a great digression and he comes back to it in Ephesians 4:1

"I the prisoner in the Lord Jesus Christ." Are you a prisoner in the Lord Jesus Christ? I think the greatest freedom in this world is the freedom to lay down your life. That is true freedom. When a man cannot lay down his life, he is bound and bound in the most terrible way of all. He wants to lay down his life, but he cannot. He wants to fall into the ground and die, but he cannot. Only the Holy Spirit coming upon you can give you the power to put to death the deeds of the body. Only the Holy Spirit can give you the power and grace to lay down your life for the Lord Jesus. It is the only way.

Subjecting Yourself One to Another

Are you prepared for the discipline? In Ephesians 5 it says, "Be filled with the Spirit; speaking one to another in psalms and hymns and spiritual songs, singing and making melody with your heart to the Lord" (vv. 18b–19). "Subjecting yourselves one to another in the fear of Christ" (v. 20b). Can you subject yourselves one to another? Not in a slavish way, not in a way that you have no personality, no spontaneity, no originality. For example: if they all look this way, you look the same way. If they all look up, you look up; if they look down, you look down. That is not subjecting yourself one to another in the fear of the Lord. It is that you accept one another in the Lord, that you respect one another in the Lord, that you reverence one another in the Lord, that you refuse whatever happens to be alienated from one another in the Lord. I think this matter of being built together is a big thing. Don't get too downcast about it. Some people say, "Oh dear, things have gone wrong. Everywhere we go we hear of fragmentation, division, etc. Let me tell you something. However much we look for something perfect down here we will never find it because God is training us and as long as that work is really being done, that is what matters.

God Produces Gold, Pearl and Precious Stones in the First Generation

When we look at church history, we find a remarkable thing. Within one generation of every move of the Spirit of God from Pentecost down to our present age the values have died. Furthermore, it appears that God is not interested in keeping something alive after the first generation. If God wanted to He could set everything in motion to keep alive the thing, but He does not. He just allows it to die. For instance, we find in nearly all the major moves since the Reformation within twenty years there have been major divisions. Lately it is the Brethren into the Exclusives and the Elders, the Puritans into the Presbyterians, Congregationalists (many of whom came here), and the Episcopalians. This is interesting because God is doing something in that first generation the values of which go into the city and are never lost. There is gold, precious stone, and pearl produced in that beginning generation and even in the second generation in that way of God which go right into the city and are never lost. God is building a city and that is why we have to learn these principles down here. We are not going to come to the throne willy-nilly. If you have not gained the victory at your kitchen sink, God is not going to bring you to the throne. If you have not gained the victory in your family, God is not going to bring you to the throne. He is not going to have people sitting on thrones who are sort of failures, who say, "I do not know what it is about this matter because I have a terrible mess in my own home." I am not saying you should be perfect in your home, and there are problems in many homes which are not of your making, but are you in the ascendancy? Are you reigning with Christ now? Are you governing things from the throne of God?

I remember the story of a brother who had in his study a big plaque on the wall which said, "Look down." And everybody who went into his study would see: "Look down." And they would say, "What do you mean, 'look down'? You generally look up." "No," he said, "it is a question of where you are. If you are seated with Christ in heavenly places, look down. Look down on everything. Don't look up; look down." It is a question of where you are.

Taking Up Responsibility

The fact of the matter is that God is teaching you values. Is God building you together? Are you learning something of the discipline of being bound together? Are you prepared in all the companies you come from to subject yourselves one to another in the Lord? Are you prepared to take responsibility? How few people take responsibility! One person will put out all the chairs, all the books, and do all the cleaning up. Everyone comes and enjoys themselves and enjoys the Lord and off they go. No one takes any responsibility, no one bothers. No one helps in the material things. The material things are what God wants you to do. They all come in, enjoy themselves and go back and say, "Who is doing the whole thing? I cannot see much enjoyment in that for me. I do not do that kind of thing." So when we truly enjoy the Lord, He will teach us in some way or other to really seek to be very practical.

Three Kinds of Wood Used in the Building

Now we have talked a lot about stones, so let us consider the wood used in the temple. If we continue on in II Chronicles 3 we find that the next thing that covers the stone is wood. The wood that was used would be of three kinds only. There was fir wood or in some versions it is cypress. I do not think it was cypress. It was much more likely to have been fir wood. Then there was cedar wood and olive wood. It seems that the great outer timbers of the ceiling and under the floor were probably fir wood. The inner wall, ceiling and floor were cedar, and the doors into the most holy place or the petition were olive wood.

Wood Symbolizes Man

In the scriptures trees always symbolize man. "Blessed is the man that walketh not in the counsel of the wicked...and he shall be like a tree planted by the streams of water" (Psalm 1:1, 3). Jeremiah says about the man who is walking with God, who trusts in God, that he is like a tree that shall not fear when drought comes. Again and again this is found in Scripture and it is the picture of humanity. Stone is rock–like, and wood is warm. Now that you have seen you are stone and you have been quarried, fitly framed together, and are in relationship together, never forget to be human beings. This is the thing where the devil undoes many a real work of God in our lives. People become spiritual machines. Oh, the spiritual machinery there is! They so suppress themselves, they so sort of feel there is something wrong with being human beings that they become a kind of walking Bible, a kind of spiritual machine. It is like a slot machine; you put in a nickel and out comes what you want. They have it all down pat. I could tell you of many, many things that I have suffered from spiritual machines.

God Never Wants Us to Lose Our Humanity

Now I want to ask you something. Was our Lord ever a spiritual machine? Never! He wept; He sorrowed; He felt; He was moved with indignation; He became angry, the whole range of human feeling was His. He was a true human without sin and was not governed by the soul. His spirit governed His soul. Once God has done a work of dividing soul and spirit in us, once our soul knows something of being broken, which is a costly business, then our soul comes into its own.

Once we begin to see what the church is, God never wants us to lose our humanity. What has happened in so many companies is that they are no longer human. When you go into them, you feel something artificial, something that is no longer human; it is like a machine. Press a button and everything flies out. That is not what God wants; He wants human beings. He wants a new man—someone who thinks, who feels, who laughs, who cries, who travails, who can be touched with the feelings of others. God loves that kind of humanity.

The Wood Used was Durable, Incorruptible, Noble

The trees which were used in the building of the temple are very interesting. First of all, fir or cypress are the most durable woods that we know, at least in the Middle East. Indeed, the Vatican has doors, some pieces of which are one thousand six hundred years old, and they are of cypress wood. That is how long it can last. There is a very old tradition that gopher wood is cypress wood. They used to make ships in the olden days of cypress because it is the most durable wood.

The cedar wood, of course, is incorruptible. If you want to have a wood in which wood-boring beetles do not get in, where dry rot does not start up and where all the other little insects and diseases do not come in, use cedar wood. Cedar wood is relatively incorruptible, and linked to that is nobility. We always think of cedar as the most aristocratic of all the trees. The Bible speaks of the great cedars of Lebanon, the king of the forest. And so we have durability, nobility, and incorruptibility. Now that is the kind of man God wants; that is the kind of humanity God wants.

Ephesians 4:24: "Put on the new man, that after God hath been created in righteousness and holiness of truth." Put on the Lord Jesus Christ, the new man. Tell me; do you find His manhood durable? Absolutely! He weathers all storms. Do you find His manhood incorruptible? He was tempted in all points like as we are yet without sin. Do you find His manhood noble? Oh, He is King of kings and Lord of lords. We find it all in Him.

The Lord is the Same Today as He was when He Walked the Earth

Now I want to ask you something else. Did you ever find the Lord Jesus acting like a machine? He said, "I do not My own works but the works of My Father; those are the ones I do. I do not speak My own words but the words of My Father." He was not a machine. He denied Himself; He acted absolutely human. I think no one could have been more human than our Lord at the tomb of Lazarus. Why did He cry at Lazarus' death?" He knew He was going to raise him from the dead. Was it an act? Was it a theatrical performance? Of course not! It was a strong word: He really wept. Why? Because of the misery all around Him. It so touched Him as to what had happened to this world, what Satan had done, what sin had done, that He cried. That is our Lord Jesus. The Lord Jesus is the same today as He was then. Just because He has gone into heaven He is not changed; He is the same yesterday, today and forever. Wonderful! He is still touched with the feelings of our infirmities. There are times when I think the Lord almost weeps. If He does not weep, He is still Man, glorified Man, as well as God.

I think of when He came to Jerusalem and He said: "O Jerusalem, Jerusalem," and He burst into tears. I believe the Lord laughs. I know people always say that we have no record of the Lord ever laughing, which probably comes from sinners who are without humor. The Pharisees could say of our Lord: "Look at

Him, He is a glutton and wine bibber." They must have seen Him at times when He was humorous as well. I cannot imagine anyone Jewish without humor. I believe He was a Man of the whole range of human feelings.

We have to be governed by the Lord; we have to be broken by the work of the cross, but we must always be human beings. Put on the new man. We have put on the new man. Let us remember in this building work not to become machinery. Let us not just become automatic. Let's not become impersonal. Don't let it all just be a press-button arrangement. Let's just be human beings. That is why God made man in the beginning to become a redeemed man. Now we are a new man in Christ. Let's never forget that. We are not just soul and spirit, and we shall never be bodyless spirits like angels. We are spirit, soul and body, redeemed by the grace of God.

In 1 Thessalonians 2:8 it says: "Even so, being affectionately desirous of you, we were well pleased to impart unto you, not the gospel of God only, but also our own souls." There is something to think about.

The Silver

Let's consider this matter of the silver? In 1 Chronicles 29:4 it says: "Even three thousand talents of gold, the gold of Ophir, and seven thousand talents of refined silver, wherewith to overlay the walls of the houses." So Bible scholars, especially the Christian ones, have had so much problem about this silver. Where is the silver? It is not mentioned in the record of the building. Yet we have over twice the amount of silver for the walls as the gold. Where did it all go? Someone said, "Well, the silver was in all the store houses. They completely lined the walls of the store houses with it. I think most of you know silver tarnishes. It would not have been a pretty sight unless they had people cleaning it regularly. Gold does not tarnish in the same way as silver; it goes quickly dark. I have found that although the Christians of old had problems with this, the rabbis never had a problem with it. They have always said, and I am sure it is true, that the silver membrane was put between the stone and the wood to stop any form of rot or trouble. I think that is probably correct. Over all the stone silver was put. Isn't that a wonderful picture of redemption?! Redemption is the only thing that will ever stop any rot. Always go back to it. Never get away from redemption. However far you go in holiness with the Lord or good works or the works that God has fore prepared that you should walk in them, really knowing something of sacrifice—never forget redemption. Neither your will nor your prayer nor your Bible knowledge nor you going on with the Lord will preserve you from rot; it is only the finished work of the Lord Jesus Christ. The only way that you will overcome Satan is by the blood of the Lamb. Go back to it again and again.

One other thing about the wood. It was carved or engraved with cherubim, lilies, palm trees and chains. First the stones were cut, then they were polished, then they were beveled, then they were fitted. Haven't we got over that stage? No, now the silver and then the wood and now the chisel again, and this time it is a work of beauty. It is the work of the cross; that is where we feel it most in our humanity. And the knife of God cuts deep because He wants to cause us in the end to show forth the excellencies of Him who called us out of darkness into His marvelous light. Is God doing that with you? Care for one another. If we know of someone going through deep waters we know the knife of God is at work in their humanity; a beautiful work of God is being wrought in them. Let's be careful and gentle. Don't stamp on the smoking flax or dimly burning wick. Let's be very gentle with those whom we know God is dealing with. Let's not smother each other with words from the Lord, but gently bear one another up in the Lord.

The Gold

Then we come to the gold. Notice that everything was overlaid with gold again and again and again. Even the nails were of gold. If you have anything to do with building, think of banging those nails of gold. It must have been quite a job because gold is a soft metal. Everything was gold. When you came into this building, you would not have known whether it was stone or silver or wood because it was all gold. You and I would be walking on a floor of gold, and it was pure gold, the best gold of all. Everything was gold. And we know that gold speaks of the divine nature. So when the stones are right and the wood is there, then the gold goes on.

I think of scriptures that say, "Christ in you, the hope of glory" (Colossians 1:27b). And in II Peter 1:4a: "Whereby he hath granted unto us his precious and exceeding great promises; that through these ye may become partakers of the divine nature." The gold is coming into us. I think of the Lord's word to the church at Laodicea: "I counsel thee." Do you want the advice of our Lord? Do you want to hear the counsel of our Lord? He said, "I counsel thee to buy of me gold refined by fire, that thou mayest become rich" (Revelation 3:18a). Gold is Christ in us the hope of glory.

Oh how wonderful it is when God has done all this work. In the end it is Christ that matters. He has to do all this preparation work, but finally it is the glory of the Lord Jesus. Don't tell me how much you know about the Bible; don't tell me how powerful you are. I want to know only one thing: Is the Lord Jesus alive in your life? That is the one thing that in the end counts, the one thing that will determine your everlasting reward in heaven. How much is there of Christ in you? John the Baptist said, "He must increase, but I must decrease" (John 3:30).

Precious Stones

Now we come to the precious stones. Finally, this gold was encrusted with precious stones. Whatever does that speak of? When you went into this house, not on the floor nor probably on the ceiling, but the walls were encrusted with beautiful precious stones that brought out the beauty of the work. There were palm trees, cherubim and lilies, and they had precious stones in special places that brought out the whole beauty of the work so that you gasped at it. If you and I walked into the house of the Lord, I think the first thing we would do is gasp. Even though we had known about it and even heard about it, we would have no idea how beautiful it was until we saw the gold everywhere.

What do these precious stones speak of? Of course, stones like these are all formed in the dark parts of the earth by heat and pressure. I think they speak of the radiance and incomparable beauties and glories of Christ. The Lord never finally shines through any saint till there has been a real work and then you begin to see this kind of thing shining out.

That is what God wants to do with you and me. I think of the scriptures that speak of the unsearchable riches of Christ: "The riches of His glory." "The riches of His grace." When you enter into the house of God, everywhere you look it is the same—the incomparable and radiant beauties and glories of Christ which are the treasures of darkness! How can you and I show forth Christ like this? Only if we are prepared to go into dark places and let God do it.

Treasures of Darkness

Let me give you two scriptures: Isaiah 45:3: "And I will give thee the treasures of darkness, and hidden riches of secret places, that thou mayest know that it is I, the Lord, who call thee by thy name, even the God of Israel."

There are treasures of darkness, hidden riches in secret places, but you have to go into those secret places where no one sees but God. And in that place something inexplicable comes into your life. Wherever I go people come to me and pour out a story and it is inexplicable. Why has the Lord done this to me? What does it all mean? How could it happen? Why me? But God is doing something, and out of that person's life comes something which could come no other way. It is something of incomparable beauty and glory and it will never be taken away.

Times of Inexplicable Suffering

Isaiah 54:11: "O thou afflicted, tossed with tempest, and not comforted, behold, I will set thy stones in fair colors, and lay thy foundations with sapphires. And I will make thy pinnacles of rubies, and they gates of carbuncles, and all thy border of precious stones."

But listen to this: "O thou afflicted, tossed with tempest, and not comforted." There are times when the Lord allows storms to come into lives and He says He will not even touch it; He is hidden. He will not even say a word; He is absolutely silent.

If I should be speaking to anyone who is in such a storm, who is in such an inexplicable way with the Lord and the Lord is absolutely silent, and you pray for a word from the Lord but He gives you none, rest in Him. You may be tossed with tempest; you may be afflicted and not comforted, but do not fear; God is doing something in your life that will shine out with incomparable beauty. He will do it; He will do it.

I remember one time in my own life when I was going through a period of great distress, and a scripture came to me by a dear old sister in the Lord who knew the Lord deeply. I could never understand why she always had in her home: "My peace I give unto thee." I used to think what a funny word that was to put up in her home: "My peace I give unto thee."

When I was in great distress, I said to her, "You know I have been in terrible torment, but suddenly I have passed into peace. I cannot tell you why because the situation is exactly as it was, but I have peace inside. "Ah," she said, "let me tell you something. Years ago when I was in great trouble, I was taken to a mental home and it seemed that nothing would help me at all." She was a lady of title, and it was a great disgrace in those days to be in a mental home. She believed in the healing of God, but He did not heal her. So she went, losing all her reputation and everything else.

She was the only Christian in her family, and she felt, "Oh, this is terrible. In great torment one verse came to me: 'Peace I leave with you, My peace I give unto you.' I saw in a flash that the Lord Jesus had left me as a legacy peace with God. He never needed that because He always had peace with God. Sin had destroyed my peace, so He left His legacy of peace to me. But His own peace was something that He, as the sinless One, found in the Garden of Gethsemane and on the cross when He said, 'Father, into Thy hands I commend Myself.' After all the torment and affliction of sorrow My peace I give unto you. I leave the other peace to you, but My peace I give unto you."

I could talk about the pillars, Jachin and Boaz, which were outside. I would like to have spoken about the cherubim. You know the old cherubim were still there over the mercy seat looking down. But the two new cherubim stood full height with wings from wall to wall and they did not look down on the mercy seat; they looked out to the house of God, and that is a lovely picture. For God must first point our attention to the finished work of the Lord Jesus Christ and then He points our attention to the habitation, a home for God in the Spirit.

Finally the house was built and the ark of the Lord came into it and the glory of the Lord filled the house. Doesn't it make that scripture live: "One thing have I desired, that will I seek after, that I may dwell in the house of the Lord all the days of my life, to behold the beauty of the Lord." You stand there and see nothing but beauty, and the wonder of it is that it is all in and through His own. What grace! It is not just the Lord Jesus uniquely Himself but revealed in those He has brought to glory with Himself, bringing many sons to glory, the presence of the Lord. In the end the habitation of God is the presence of the Lord. He wants to commit Himself.

Where is God at Home?

Some of your versions probably say, "The staves were drawn out." Others say the staves were lengthened, or others say the staves were made longer. We have a great problem because in the Hebrew it just says, "The staves were made longer." How can you make staves longer? No one could understand this. What I think it probably means is that the staves were drawn half out because the law of Moses forbade that the staves should ever be taken out (see Exodus 25:15). So they were probably drawn half out to signify that the ark had come home. No more traveling. And probably the poles came out lengthened and you could just see the bulge of them from the holy place. That is how you would see from the tent of meeting just the ends of the staves, probably pushing out to show people that God is at home; at last God is at home.

Oh, wherever I go I hear, "Where is God at home?" Is He at home here in Richmond, va? Is He at home in Washington? Is He at home in Richmond, Surry? Is He at home in these other places? Where is God at home? There are thousands of living stones, many, many dear believers with real experience of the Lord, but where has the ark come home? Where are the staves being lengthened that God has finally come home?

And so we can end with that scripture from Psalm 27: "One thing have I asked of the Lord, that will I seek after, that I may dwell in the house of the Lord all the days of my life, to behold the beauty of the Lord, and to inquire in His temple" (v. 4).

Seeing the beauty of the Lord will bring sacrifices of praise unto Him, and something of His glory will be manifested in the saints who are being changed together into His likeness from glory to glory. Inquiring in His temple is real service. That is what the house of God is for. First, it is for the presence of the Lord, secondly it is for worship, thirdly, it is that we may be changed from glory to glory, fourthly, it is that we may serve Him, inquiring of the Lord. May the Lord bless you.

Other books by Lance Lambert

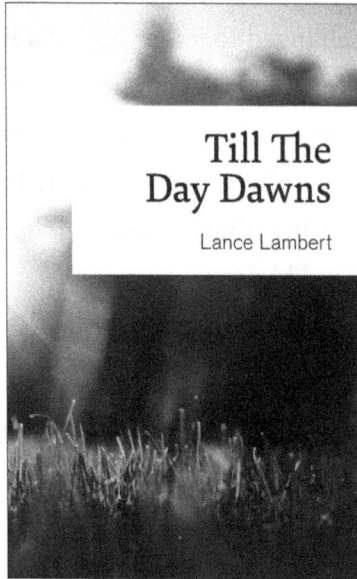

Till the Day Dawns

"And we have the word of prophecy made more sure; whereunto ye do well that ye take heed, as unto a lamp shining in a dark place, until the day dawn, and the day-star arise in your hearts." (II Peter 1:9).

The word of prophecy was not given that we might merely be comforted but that we would be prepared and made ready. Let us look into the Word of God together searching out the prophecies, that the Day-Star arise in our hearts until the Day dawns.

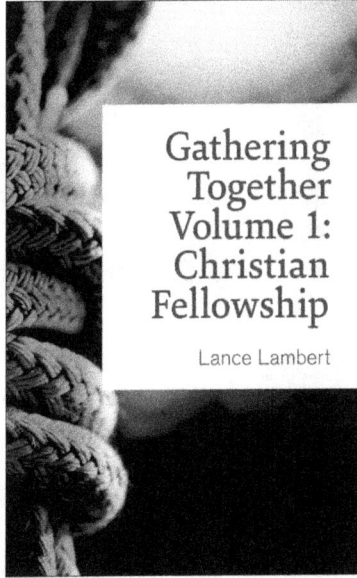

Gathering Together

What is the church?

What is the basis for meeting together as the church?

What is true fellowship?

What is the priesthood of all believers?

What is the difference between unity
and uniformity in the church?

In this book, the first volume of *Gathering Together*, Lance
Lambert answers these questions and many more. In doing this,
he emphasizes the absolute headship of Christ and the oneness of
the body of Christ.

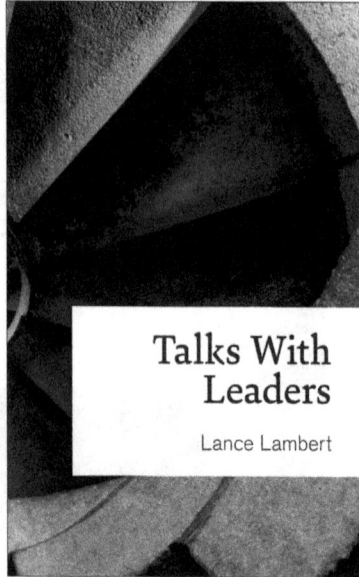

Talks With Leaders

"O Timothy, guard that which is committed unto thee ..."
(1 Timothy 6:20) Has God given you something? Has God
deposited something in you? Is there something of Himself
which He has given to you to contribute to the people of God?
Guard it. Guard that vision which He has given you. Guard that
understanding that He has so mercifully granted to you. Guard
that experience which He has given that it does not evaporate or
drain away or become a cause of pride. Guard that which the Lord
has given to you by the Holy Spirit. In these heart-to-heart talks
with leaders Lance Lambert covers such topics as the character
of God's servants, the way to serve, the importance of anointing,
and hearing God's voice. Let us consider together how to remain
faithful with what has been entrusted to us.